IMAGE MATTERS!

First Steps on the Journey to Your Best Self

dear Paul,
Best wishes
along your journey
Cheers
Lauren
5/05

Lauren Solomon

Education/Exposure Publications
New York, New York

Published by Education/Exposure Publications
2124 Broadway, Suite 197
New York, NY 10023

Publisher's Cataloging-in-Publication Data
Solomon, Lauren.
    Image matters!: first steps on the journey to your best self / Lauren Solomon.-New York, NY: Education/Exposure Publications, 2002.

    p.; cm.
    ISBN 0-9708608-0-3
    1. Self-perception. 2. Body image. 3. Self-actualization (Psychology). I. Title.

BF697.5 .S43 S65   2002   2002101508
158.1   --dc21   CIP

06 05 04 03 02 • 5 4 3 2 1

Project coordination by Jenkins Group, Inc. • www.bookpublishing.com
Cover and book design by Theresa Burau-Baehr
Cover photography by Ken Lull
Cover makeup by Duane Sevelin

Printed in the United States of America

This book is for my family.

For my parents, Cookie and Marty, who never tried to force my visions into little boxes but instead encouraged me to dream.

For my brother, Steven, who shares my joy, my struggles, and my belief that family is everything and all whom you love are family.

IMAGE MATTERS!

First Steps on the Journey to Your Best Self

What's Inside

Welcome! xv
1—Your Self **01**
Your Self Image 02
Your Purpose 04
Your Attitude 06
Your Style 10
Your Choices 13
Start Today! 15
For More Inspiration, Discovery, and Ideas 15
2—Your Appearance **17**
Your Wardrobe 19
Your Routine 23
Your Colors 27
Your Make-up 31
Your Hair 33
Your Hygiene 35
Start Today! 36
For More Inspiration, Discovery, and Ideas 36
3—Your Physical Health **39**
Your Family Health History and Your Habits 42
Your Fitness and Nutrition 43
Start Today! 45
For More Inspiration, Discovery, and Ideas 46
4—Your Home **47**
Your Space 49
Your Surroundings 52
Start Today! 54
For More Inspiration, Discovery, and Ideas 54
5—Your Relationships **55**
Your Propellers, Maintainers, and Drainers 55
Start Today! 59
For More Inspiration, Discovery, and Ideas 59

What's Inside (con't)

6—Your Social Self **61**
Your Public Persona 61
Start Today! 64
For More Inspiration, Discovery, and Ideas 64
7—Your Work **67**
Your Passion 68
Your Work/Your Self 71
The Brand Called You 72
Start Today! 75
For More Inspiration, Discovery, and Ideas 75
Instant Image Matters! **79**

Acknowledgements

Every book is the work of many hearts and minds.

My deepest thanks to…

My best girlfriends, Susan, Katrina, Gayle, Ann Marie, and Will, all of whom sat at one time or another on my living room floor and helped me dream, shared my vision, never judged or at least painfully held their tongues.

My AICI family who share with me, who inspire me, who challenge me and push me beyond my limits every day: Q, Chris, Louise, Jennifer, Carolyn, Jean, Helena, Jon, Penny, Holly, Anna, Nancy, Marion, and Catherine.

My friends and family from Chemical/Chase who trusted me enough to invite me into their lives, and often into their closets: Roberta, Jack, John, Carol, Pat, Frances, Liz, Elizabeth, and Meryl.

My NYU Executive MBA '93 classmates and MDarling who showed me that I could live what I love. Joanne, Marty, Michael, and Andy who would laugh with me, never at me.

Interns and friends who gave me the gift of their time to create the space in my life needed for this book to grow—Diane, Debra, Kerry, Lisa, and Jessica.

Clients who have given me the joy of a lifetime and a heart much fuller than I ever knew I could possess.

And finally, to Joel, Jerry, and Diana who saw the potential and encouraged me to begin.

A Note on Clients' Stories

The stories included in this book are composites designed to underscore important points and show the Image Matters! principles in action. Any resemblance to a single person or situation is purely coincidental.

I sit on the edge of the king-sized bed, a curious nine-year-old peering into my mother's bathroom as she gets ready for a Saturday night out with my father. I wince as she puts an eyelash curler to her lashes and watch in amazement as she inserts her lashes between the rubber pads, gently squeezes and stops to inspect the arc of the perfect curl she's created.

She draws delicate lines on her lids using a cake of black eye paint and a moistened brush, and applies the finishing touches to her face. Humming a favorite tune along with the radio, she passes me on the way to her closet, smiling lightly. A hint of Chanel No. 5 follows her. She reaches for the shoes and matching handbag already chosen and at the ready on her dresser.

I dash to the front stoop where the neighborhood kids play, riding bicycles and jumping rope in the cul-de-sac. My parents stand ready to depart at the top of the stoop. My mother pauses to remind my brother and me to behave for the sitter, adding the age-old parental warning: "Don't open the door for strangers."

The street games stop, and for a moment, everything moves in slow motion. All eyes are on my parents, especially my mother. What's she wearing? Where are they going tonight?

She is elegant, perfectly coordinated (even my father's ensemble is coordinated with hers), composed, and self aware. I sigh softly, filled with a sense of pride as if I had somehow personally created this vision of a woman.

She descends the stairs on my father's arm, comfortable with who she is, ready to savor whatever the evening has in store.

* * *

The care and pleasure my mother took in preparing to leave the house, no matter what the occasion, has stayed with me all these years. She thoughtfully designed her look, her behavior (always a gift in hand when visiting friends or family), her relationships, and her home to reflect the person and the life she envisioned for herself, and by extension, for her family.

In this most informal yet influential classroom—my childhood home—I learned about the courage and the dedication it takes to look at yourself, your life, and your world and to do the work to design them to fulfill your vision.

Who would have thought that after years of formal education and experience, I would find my way back to a seed planted so long ago? A seed that grew into an understanding that my vision of myself will take me exactly where I want to go—if I let it.

This is my ultimate message, and my gift to you.

—Lauren

Welcome!

"Your image is your most important communications tool. It tells the world who you are and who you want to be. Cultivate your image deliberately and strategically, and all doors will open before you."

Imagine getting up every morning filled with joyful anticipation of the day. You look in the mirror and feel peaceful and pleased. You see more than a reflection of your face. You see a reflection of your life. You see your creation: your space, your time, your style, your relationships, your work.

As you savor a cup of coffee at your kitchen table, you zero-in on the day's details.

Your morning, your day, in fact your whole life, reflects your personal best.

Over time, you consciously envisioned your personal best and designed your message. You built a wardrobe that works and relationships that support you. You learned how to use nutrition and fitness as tools to create more energy and vitality in your life.

Who *is* this person enjoying such a calm, organized, brilliant life...inside and out?

It is the potential in each and every one of us—man, woman, young professional, working parent, married, single, retired—to envision success, to fulfill our dreams, to grow...to move deliberately, thoughtfully, and joyfully in the direction of our personal best.

I believe in this person because I believe in you.

Inside Out or Outside In

You are about to embark on a journey. Destination: your best self. Duration: the rest of your life. This unending journey of self-discovery will give you the tools to define and refine the way you think about yourself, the image you project to the world, and how the world receives you.

This journey will create your life, if you let it.

And it begins with your image.

We sometimes get hung up on the notion of *image*. It sounds external, superficial, even shallow. My personal philosophy is that your image is an energy force that both fills and surrounds you, one with internal and external connections.

Inside, there's your vision of your self, your passions, your aspirations. Outside, there's your appearance, the relationships you nurture, the quality of your communication, your health, the home you create, your career.

Clearly, image is multi-dimensional; it embraces all that we are and all that we do...and *image matters in all we do.*

We also get stuck on the idea that the root of personal transformation must be internal; that the first thing we must change is our minds. We think that until we change our minds, we can't change anything else. We insist that change is fundamentally an "inside" job.

Many well-intentioned and highly motivated people have gotten caught in this one-dimensional thinking, only to throw up their hands in defeat with an exasperated: "Forget it! I'll always see myself as that chubby kid in grammar school who couldn't hit a baseball if his life depended on it," or "I'm basically disorganized and will always have a clutter problem," or "I can't wear make-up; I feel like a clown."

In fact, since this journey has many dimensions (your internal vision, your appearance, communication, behavior, surroundings, relationships, physical health and chosen profession are all facets of it), everyone's starting point is unique and personal.

For some, internal change is indeed essential. For others, a physical "makeover" is a comfortable place to begin. Still others are content to work on one external dimension at a time, relationships, or physical surroundings for instance. Men may choose to concentrate first on their work, while women as a group may tend more in the direction of appearance.

Once you realize that there are many starting points and paths to take, you see the many options for how, when, and where to begin the process. The point that feels best for you is the perfect point for you to embark on your unique and personal journey.

Consider that in the space of a single hour, you can—
- get a fresh haircut or buy a new pair of shoes
- eat a healthful meal
- enjoy an invigorating walk
- reconnect with a former colleague on the phone
- clean out that box of "stuff" that's been sitting in your den for six months

Each simple act instantly generates new thoughts, boosts your confidence, and helps you envision new possibilities. Simply by taking one step that changes how you spend a single hour of your life, you've set out on your journey to your best self. You've moved beyond an old limitation or discarded an element of your image that no longer fits. You've replaced an ineffectual habit with an empowering one. One at a time, these new choices and actions transform your image and your life.

You've set out on the lifelong journey to discover and create your best self.

* * *

Because there are an unlimited number of ways to start and continue on your journey, **IMAGE MATTERS!** is designed to make everyone feel welcome.

Start with a journey from the inside-out, using **Chapter 1: Your Self** (*Your Self Image, Your Purpose, Your Attitude, Your Style, Your Choices*). Or, embark upon your journey from the outside-in beginning with **Chapter 2: Your Appearance** (*Your Wardrobe, Your Routine, Your Colors, Your Make-up, Your Hair, Your Hygiene*).

Dive straight into the middle with **Chapter 5: Your Relationships** (*Your Propellers, Maintainers, and Drainers*). Or begin at the end with **Quick Start: Instant Image Matters!**

If you have the time, read from start to finish, practicing the ideas and suggestions as you go. Or try the simple steps at the end of each section. And, be sure to look into some of the books and resources I've listed at the end of each Chapter in the section called *For More Inspiration, Discovery, and Ideas.*

IMAGE MATTERS! is yours. Tackle as much as you can, when you can, and remember that even the smallest change will open doors and begin to pave the way.

Now, off you go – Enjoy!

Tools for the Journey

IMAGE MATTERS! is a philosophy and a lifelong process of visualization and transformation. At the heart of this process—this journey—is something I call your *Me File™*, a "for-your-eyes-only" activity book that houses images and ideas about your self—past, present, and future.

Your lifelong journey to your personal best will have twists and turns, challenges and celebrations, new jobs, new homes, and old and new friends. Through it all, the disciplined use of your *Me File* will reveal an important story: the story of your growth, achievements, and earned wisdom, as well as proof of your strength, creativity, and resourcefulness. You'll see that your personal best isn't a destination, something you strive to reach "one day." Rather, it's a story of becoming. Every day, every hour, every decision you make, every action you take brings what's positive, fulfilling, and enriching to you.

As you work through this process, you'll fill this *Me File* with images of a physical, financial, material, and spiritual vision of yourself borrowed from magazines, your personal photo collection, and your imagination…your vision of your self as you are and as you intend to be. This vision and the hopes and the dreams it represents will change over time, and you'll need to refresh the images in your *Me File*. Since your *Me File* is both historical and visionary, it should offer you flexibility and room to grow. For this reason, a three-ring binder works best.

I suggest choosing or creating a binder that's visually appealing to you, rather than a reminder of pop quizzes and college papers. Select a vibrant color or cover a plain-vanilla binder in a fabric with a pattern and texture you love to make it both a visual and tactile experience, a part of this process that you deeply enjoy and look forward to.

Be sure to date all your entries so you can note your growth and progression. Add folders that have pockets or plastic sleeves that will hold random images and photographs until you have time to sort through them, attach them to a page in the book, and weave them into the story of your journey.

You'll also need—
- scissors
- a glue stick or tape
- a variety of magazines
- family photos: you alone (all ages), you with family and friends, even those dreaded senior prom pictures!
- pens, in a variety of sizes, textures, and colors
- filler paper, in a rainbow of colors

Your *Me File* is physical evidence of the energy you are investing in your growth and evolution to your personal best. It's a visual journey with you at the controls, proof that you're taking an active part in creating your image and your life, living by design and on purpose.

Your Self

YOUR MIND'S MIRROR

If you're an avid reader of personal growth books, chances are you've heard the claim that our thoughts determine our circumstances. In fact, the power of thought is a consistent theme and often the defining principle in these valuable texts.

The reason is simple: it is the truth.

"There is nothing worse than a brilliant image of a fuzzy concept."

–Ansel Adams,
American artist, photographer

The mind's mirror—the way we envision ourselves in our own minds—is far more powerful and influential than anything in the fitting room in any department store. It controls our thoughts, our actions, the choices we make, our preferences, desires, hopes, and beliefs about all that is possible.

That's not to say that change *must* begin on the inside. On the contrary, experience has taught me that personal transformation can certainly start on the outside. A new job, a new relationship, a brand new look or other "external change" can serve to generate the momentum and excitement needed to set the journey in motion.

The process of creating your best self is not necessarily a straight line from the inside out. Rather, it's a spiral upward, one with a definite beginning, but no end. Each turn of the spiral brings awakenings and discoveries that teach you, influence the way you think, change the choices you make, alter your passions, shift your commitment to certain relationships, improve your appearance, impact your total health, and more.

Bear in mind however, that your internal image is a vital companion and a powerful ally on this journey. Hold it in high regard, honor it, and respect it for its power and influence.

The self you see in your head is the self you will share with the world. When you truly appreciate the strength of this image, you become responsible for its contents and its quality. You know that everything—your choices, attitudes, relationships, even your physical surroundings—are an external expression of the image you see reflected in your mind's mirror.

YOUR SELF IMAGE

Jack

Jack weighed 200 pounds at the age of 13. He is now 32, and his weight is appropriate to his height and build. But in his own mind, he's still the chubby boy, the brunt of his classmates' jokes. He avoids parties, has few dates and hesitates to speak up in business meetings...anything to avoid the spotlight where he might once again experience the unkind remarks and rejection he endured so many years ago.

Jack and I worked together to update the reflection he saw in his mind's mirror, but this image already cost him almost two decades of joy, excitement, adventure, and personal growth. This is the power of the picture in your mind...left unchecked, it will stand in your way forever.

Picture Me What's reflected in your mind's mirror? It's worth a close look since, like Jack, we all make choices, both consciously and unconsciously, that attract events and circumstances into our lives. This reflection is slowly but surely guiding every aspect of your life. It is a template for the way you live.

Your Self

How do you see yourself? Most people couldn't say. Their internal vision is jumbled and confused, or so terribly narrow that no clear picture emerges.

To help my clients bring these images into focus, I adapted the following *Picture Me* activity from the work of my colleagues, certified professional image consultants, Dominique Isbecque and Jennifer Parkinson.

1. Take your *Me File*, supplies and magazine and photo collection into a quiet corner (no phone, e-mail or TV!).

2. Select pictures that represent how you see yourself today. What images accurately represent the total picture you have of yourself in the present? How do you envision your appearance (covered head to toe in ribbons and lace or strictly jeans and T-shirts?), your home (neat as a pin, messy as a college dorm or perhaps something in between?), your activities (mostly sports, social, volunteer work or a combination?), your job (leading meetings or on the phone all day?), etc.

    Next, find images that depict the person you'd like to be. How would you like your life to look? What activities would make you feel good, excited, happy, and eager? What outfits would help you to walk confidently into your next staff meeting or joyfully anticipate your next Saturday night out? Is there a hairstyle you've always wanted to try...maybe something radical that always seemed too daring for you? Find images of people who appear outgoing and funny or reserved and pensive, depending on the direction in which you'd like to travel.

3. Attach all these images to the pages in your *Me File* and make some notes.
    Me-Now Images
    - What do I like about this picture?
    - What would I change?
    - How did I feel about this picture?
    - How would I like to feel about this picture?

    Me-To-Be Images
    - What attracted me to this picture? Is it the look? The feeling? The setting?
    - In what specific ways does this image differ from Me-Now?
    - What steps could I take to bring this activity, look, job, etc. into my life?

Image Matters!

The *Picture Me* activity is often a decisive first step in becoming aware of your internal image and envisioning a positive, fulfilling future.

Simply by selecting images and reflecting on your attraction to them, you get information that empowers you to create a strategy for aligning your internal image with your external one, and vice versa...a strategy uniquely suited to your journey.

You begin to relax into a self image and personal style that are fully aligned...inside and out. You consciously and unconsciously begin to move in the direction of your dreams, making decisions and choices that bring that new person into the present and begin to reveal, first to you and then to the world, your authentic, true, and personal best.

Perhaps the most important lesson to derive from the *Picture Me* activity is that *you* are in control because you—and only you—can change the image in your mind.

Only you can design and present your best message, your best self.

YOUR PURPOSE

How would you characterize your day's activities? Are they merely routine, the "same stuff, different day?" Or is each day exciting and new, a daring adventure? What is your purpose?

Try this:

> Imagine for a moment that you are a Benedictine monk living in the Middle Ages. Your life is one of purpose and focus. You own nothing, having renounced all personal property when you entered the order. Your days are organized around study, prayer (you pray seven times a day and once at night), meals, meetings, and manual labor as a spiritual quest. Your work is precise and holy. You have been taught to "treat everything as if it were a vessel of the altar." You see yourself as a temporary steward of the world, which is a holy creation.

Purpose is the organizing principle of your life. You are on earth to praise and exalt God, and each day is planned to the minute in exquisite detail toward the fulfillment of this mission. Your purpose gives your life meaning, structure, and something more: it enables you to find peace in an age of constant turmoil, surrounded by disease, famine, and perpetual warfare.

> *"The purpose of life is a life of purpose."*
>
> —*Robert Byrne, author and columnist*

Is it any wonder that the Benedictine Monks produced art, architecture, metalworks, and textiles of such quality and value that their influence endures many hundreds of years later? Even today, Benedictine products are synonymous with craftsmanship, timeless beauty, and lasting quality.

This is the power of purpose and its deep connection to your inner image and its outer expression.

Travel Your Journey with Purpose

What is your purpose? Here are some ways my clients and students have responded to this life-affirming question—

- "I want to raise happy, healthy children."
- "I want to feel satisfied in my work and have plenty of time to be with my family."
- "I want to return to a simple, uncomplicated way of life."
- "I want to help others, not focus on myself all the time."
- "I want to make a difference in the world."

Notice that at the heart of everyone's purpose is a mission that benefits someone or something else. We all hope to have some sort of impact on

5

the world, to create something wonderful, and to leave a legacy, whether that legacy is our children, a novel, paintings, a business, or a good name.

And, while it may feel strange to be asked, "What's your purpose?" realize it's incredibly simple in the long run: we all want to make a difference of some kind.

So, what is your purpose? Take out your *Me File* and begin writing the past achievements that you value most in your life. Why do you attach importance to these achievements? What lessons have they taught you and what do these lessons tell you about your purpose, the impact you want to have on the world, the legacy you want to leave behind, the activities and accomplishments that will make you jump out of bed in the morning, ready to tackle the day with joy, spirit, and energy? What goals will give your life a sense of meaning, purpose, and value? Record all your answers in your *Me File*.

Copy these sentence stems in your *Me File* and then fill in the blanks:

- I believe in

  _____

- I am grateful for

  _____

- Today had purpose because

  _____

- Tomorrow, I will

  _____

- Next week, I will

  _____

- I am most proud of

  _____

- I want my days to feel

  _____

- At the end of each day, I want to feel

  _____

Once you are clear about your purpose, every day is exciting. Suddenly, you're living your life according to the knowledge that every day takes you closer to its fulfillment. Trends and fads are no longer real temptations or serious diversions. They are, at most, interesting interludes. You are traveling your journey with purpose.

YOUR ATTITUDE

Attitude, at its core, is simply a matter of perspective. You've heard the cliché: you can see the glass as you choose: half empty or half full. You can be aggravated about the traffic jam, or grateful that you've got a car that works. Disappointed about being passed over for a promotion, or thrilled to have been considered. Upset that a relationship ended or happy to be free to pursue future relationships.

"You can complain because roses have thorns or rejoice because thorns have roses."

—*Ziggy, cartoon character and beloved purveyor of simple wisdom*

The word *attitude* is synonymous with *mindset, outlook,* and *viewpoint.* To me, mindset is the most expressive of these synonyms because it suggests habitual ways of thinking and reacting to circumstances. Attitude is absolutely a habit, and it can be your greatest asset or your greatest liability, as Nicolas' story illustrates…

Nicolas

I met Nicolas on a train traveling from Washington, D.C. to New York City. In four hours, I had not only heard Nicolas' story, I had become a part of it. Nicolas had come to the United States as a young man to study. He fully intended to complete his studies and return to his country to work, marry, and raise a family. Through his talent, dedication, and drive, Nicolas had impressed his professors and was offered and accepted multiple opportunities to remain and work in the U.S.

Image Matters!

At first he was elated.

But as time passed, Nicolas became resentful, angry, and frustrated that opportunities in his own country were neither as plentiful nor as rewarding. He wanted to go home, but to what? He felt trapped in the U.S. He began to broadcast his feelings to friends, colleagues…anyone within earshot. Nicolas became negative, disillusioned, and rigid, even argumentative. Eventually, no one would work with him. His reputation and career were in danger. Even his friends began avoiding his company.

As Nicolas shared his story with me, he told me that he had just spent the weekend with a friend who invited him to Washington in order to confront him with the hard truth. The friend said that Nicolas' attitude had soured and that he was damaging his own life—present and future. Through the words of this brave and caring friend, Nicolas finally awakened to the ways in which his attitude was limiting his life.

We continued our conversation over coffee at the train station when we arrived in New York. I asked Nicolas to describe his life now and to create a picture of the life he envisioned as ideal. Nicolas' description of his ideal life was very close to the life he currently had, except it was in the wrong location and it lacked a loving partner, since his negativity had severely hampered his ability to meet a woman who would consider spending an evening, much less her entire life, with him.

Nicolas and I became fast friends and continued to work together for some time after. Along the way he also sought the counsel of other professional advisors to assist in the hard work of changing his mindset about his ability to build the rich, fulfilling life he dreamed of.

Life quickly accommodated his new positive vision with opportunities and experiences that aligned with his dreams.

Today, Nicolas is in the process of establishing a bi-national project for his company, which will enable him to work part-time in his country and part-time in the U.S. While it's not yet an ideal situation, his attitude has once again shifted from despair to hopeful action. Rather than letting his attitude limit his life, Nicolas is motivated to return to his original outlook toward a positive future of his own creation.

You Belong to the World

There is perhaps no single more important realization to grasp than this: your attitude colors your perceptions and shapes your responses to every experience you encounter along your journey.

As I tell my clients and students, from the moment you leave your home in the morning, you belong to the world. An open, enlightened attitude enables you to see the world and the world to see your authentic self. A negative attitude, on the other hand, costs the world twice. Once by preventing you from knowing the world and again by preventing the world from knowing you.

Copy these sentence stems in your *Me File* and then fill in the blanks:

- I am happiest when

    _____

- I smile most when

    _____

- I feel beautiful/attractive when

    _____

- I am fulfilled when

    _____

- I like myself most when

    _____

- I feel at ease when

    _____

The Power of Attitude

You can't hide it. Your attitude speaks volumes about you, your values, desires, and dreams. It broadcasts a clear image and message about you to the world, whether you want it to or not. Your attitude radiates from a place deep inside you, and its energy is so powerful that people will sense it before you have spoken even one word.

Image Matters!

When I became the Vice President of Professional Image Development at Chase Manhattan Bank, I believed the world had grown a halo. I thoroughly loved my job. It was the realization of a dream I had been afraid to dream. It seemed unreasonably bold and impossible at the time. I had been given the opportunity to create—from nothing—a department fully devoted to employee image development within a mega-organization.

I was happy—make that *ecstatic*—from the moment I woke up until I turned out the last light at night. I wore a natural smile that came from the depths of my being. Until then, I had never felt better, performed better, or communicated more clearly without a word just how fulfilled and happy I was.

My attitude of joy and sense of purpose were enough to fill me and the space around me. You can't fake this sort of heartfelt joy and honest contentment...no matter how good an actor you are. Complete strangers would stop me in the elevator to ask where I worked. When I told them, they'd want to know if they could come to work for me. Some said they had never met anyone who truly loved their job and radiated that love the way I did.

This is the power of attitude. Think strategically about this remarkable tool, make it an asset on your journey. When you do, you will feel great, look great...and radiate your greatness each day.

I don't know anyone who would refuse an offer like that!

YOUR STYLE

What words come to mind when you think of Jacqueline Kennedy Onassis? Nearly everyone answers with words like elegance, class, grace, sophistication, style. In fact she is widely considered a paragon of personal style, and probably will be for years to come.

There was a calm predictability to her appearance. She wore her inside on the outside. Though they may have changed slightly from time to time,

10

her clothes, make-up, accessories, and hairstyle were consistent, timeless, and classic. No matter what the occasion or time of year, every element of her appearance was carefully planned to present an image of class and sophistication. Her style was her message.

> *"Fashion can be bought. Style one must possess."*
>
> —*Edna Woolman Chase, former Editor U.S. Vogue Magazine*

She put everyone around her at ease because her visual style, her appearance, was an external expression of her personal style. The consistency in her style gave others a sense of security and drew people to her. Her total commitment to her message and her style bred familiarity. We felt we knew her.

There was, in fact, such integrity between her self and her style that her image became synonymous with her name and continues its powerful influence to this day. She was class, she was grace…she was Jackie O.

Your Turn How would you characterize your personal style? Is it classic, sporty, professional, vintage, trendy? Is it a genuine reflection of your authentic self? Is it consistent with your purpose, your attitude, and your passions? Or are there some inconsistencies that need adjusting?

Sara

Consider Sara, a university professor with a two-year-old daughter at home. Sara came to see me wearing well-worn jeans, a denim shirt, and loafers. She explained that neither her students nor her colleagues accorded her the respect she deserved.

Sara's *Picture Me* activity helped her to see the image she was projecting to her colleagues, her students, and the world. The photos she selected

11

depicted country settings with fields of flowers and children playing. People were almost always dressed casually, kicking back, sipping lemonade.

Sara's image of herself was inconsistent with her colleagues' and students' expectations of an urban university professor.

She began to realize that she needed to adjust her style to convey her authority, maturity, and expertise. Her hope, as she explained to me, was that she might be able to accomplish this without sacrificing the comfort she valued and had grown accustomed to.

Sara also felt a strong need for some degree of consistency between her image at work and her image at home. As she put it, "I don't want to be two people. They're both me. It's important that the two 'me's' work together."

So we began with some simple changes. In place of jeans and denim shirts, Sara agreed to purchase lightweight wool trousers in navy and gray and pair them with simple cotton knit tops. Her loafers worked for her desired message and style. She started to buy silk knit sweater sets that afforded her a number of easy looks that were versatile and very comfortable and found that she could add some simple touches, a belt or a pin, that she especially liked in order to personalize her look further.

In the process of refreshing her image with the aim of being accorded the respect and recognition she desired, Sara was thrilled that she didn't have to lose the comfort or consistency she valued.

Together we also realized that Sara had become accustomed to speaking to a two-year-old. The soft, sing-song tone and pace of her speech weren't well-received by her students who had begun to feel a bit alienated and patronized. Once Sara recognized the need to speak with more authority in a tone and cadence more appropriate to her audience, she sharpened her message and completed the picture.

A variety of factors including your wardrobe, your attitude, even your tone of voice all work together to create a personal style that is as unique as a fingerprint. Like Jackie O's hair and clothes, like Coco Chanel's signature red lipstick, your style reflects you.

Each of us has unique elements of our style...whether in the way we dress, speak, or style our hair. These are clearly part of who we are inside. They are aspects of our authentic selves we can't help but actively show on the outside.

Personal style sends a consistent and unwavering message that gives others the comfort and confidence to know what to expect when you enter the room.

Style is an external expression of your inner substance: your purpose, your passion, your choices. Style is the way you, and only you, put all this together...strategically and systematically throughout your journey to your best self.

YOUR CHOICES

Joanne

Joanne called me searching for someone she could trust to help her change her image. She was a 50-something single mother of three grown children, grandmother of two, and a professional and highly skilled specialist in her field. She had recently been promoted to a senior position and felt old, frumpy and out of shape...unable to project a powerful, poised, and assertive image to her new staff and peers.

Joanne's closing line to me on the phone was, "I just look awful. How can I get help?"

Joanne's *Picture Me* activity revealed that the last time she liked the way she looked was 25 years earlier, when she was the mother of toddlers, waif thin and, in her mind, vibrant. Fast forward 25 years to find Joanne 40 pounds heavier, professionally successful...and most definitely vibrant, though not in her own mind.

Image Matters!

Joanne's journey began with a great big reality check and new understanding of the value of age and experience. We began by discussing a quote from PLUS STYLE *(Penguin Books, 1996),* a book by my colleague and friend, Suzan Nanfeldt: "You can learn to look in the mirror and like what you see."

That seemed incredible to Joanne at first, but she had a secret strength: she had decided to change her life.

The rest was easy.

She began her journey fully committed to embracing the process of aligning her style with her vision of her best self.

Joanne quickly realized that she didn't like being so far from the Colorado country home she loved and the family members who were her emotional pillars of support. She decided to stop doing what others expected of her and listen instead to her own heart. Joanne left her very corporate, cosmopolitan life to live and work full-time in the country.

She began working with a medical specialist on her weight and has since adopted a regime of daily walks and other moderate exercise.

Her look today—less than one year into her personal journey—is that of a woman who has chosen to live the life she imagined.

"It's so hard when I have to, and so easy when I want to."

—*Sondra Anice Barnes, author*

Choosing is but a mental game of solitaire until a choice is translated into action. Take a few moments to think about your choices and the actions that support them.

What choices have you made, neglected to make, or successfully avoided? Which of these have you energetically acted on? Which have remained merely decision points in your mind? What do these choices and actions say about you, your attitude, your purpose, your image and vision for your life?

Record the answers in your *Me File.*

START TODAY!

Begin a *Me File* (see pages XXI-XXII for an explanation).
1.   Clip photos that reflect how you see yourself today. Attach these to the pages in your *Me File* and date your entry.
2.   Clip photos that reflect your vision of your best self. Attach these to the pages in your *Me File.*
3.   On the next page in your *Me File,* write five differences you notice between the two.
4.   Next, list five steps you can take to bring your current self closer to your vision of your best self.
5.   Tackle one at a time until you find that you've successfully completed all the previous steps.

FOR MORE INSPIRATION, DISCOVERY, AND IDEAS

*   *Creative Visualization: Use the Power of Your Imagination to Create What You Want in Your Life* by Shakti Gawain, Bantam Starfire, 1983
*   *The Artist's Way: A Spiritual Path to Higher Creativity* by Julia Cameron, JP Tarcher, 1992
*   *Life Makeovers* by Cheryl Richardson, Broadway Books, 2000

2 Your Appearance

The inimitable Mae West. Born in Brooklyn, New York on August 17, 1893, Mae began her film career in 1932 after appearing for years as a child star in Vaudeville. In addition to building a successful film career, Mae wrote a number of plays, including the highly successful *Diamond Lil* which became a full-length film in which she had her first starring role.

> *"It's not what I say, but how I say it; and it's not what I do, but how I do it; and it's how I look when I say and do it."*
>
> — *Mae West, actress, playwright, and, I'd like to think, Image Matters! pioneer*

By the time she retired from the cinema in the early 1940s, Mae had nine movies to her credit. Her popularity had saved Paramount Pictures from bankruptcy.

Mae was audacious, sassy, classy, irreverent, and risqué. A vital and independent voice in a country living through the Depression years.

It was her complete confidence and sense of herself that caused her to stand out and to remain, so many years later, a model of unflappable self-awareness. She had a very definite sense of style and sense of herself. She knew how to draw people to her.

She also knew intuitively that "how she looked when she said and did it" was hugely important. People make decisions about us based on our wardrobe, make-up, hair, grooming...every element of physical appearance, whether we want them to or not.

And that in many ways, these "nonverbal" cues say more than words ever could.

From the Outside In

Contrary to popular thought, it's neither shallow nor pointless to concentrate on your appearance. Along the journey to your best self and forever after, appearance communicates on two levels. Both will fuel the journey. First, your choices about your appearance speak to you. Then, they speak about you to the world around you.

Think about how you feel sporting that new crisp suit and tie, holding an immaculate briefcase in which you're carrying your well-written resume and best work samples. You stand tall, shoulders back without apparent effort. You're clear-headed, focused, and ready. *You feel sharp because you look sharp.*

The reason you reach for comfortable clothes on a Saturday is not only that you want to feel comfortable, but you want to be in a frame of mind that says, "I'm not doing business now." In your favorite well-worn jeans and cotton shirt, it's easy to put your feet up, enjoy a long breakfast, read the paper cover to cover, and enjoy relaxing time with friends and family. Later, you'll organize your errands and chores so you can hit the ground running on Monday.

Of course, your choices about every facet of your appearance communicate to the rest of the world, but first, they speak to you. Thus, they have a direct and powerful influence on how you feel. When you present your best to the world, you begin to feel at your best in the world. This is one of the reasons I urge clients and students to begin the journey wherever they are...ready for a journey inward or outward. If sprucing up your appearance is the best way for you to begin, by all means, start there!

"Does this look okay?"

Whether the question refers to lipstick, new shoes, an outfit or haircut, it seems I hear it every day. Most people are hoping to hear a response of, "Yes!"

But here's a much better question: "Do I look my best? Is this the best I can do right now?" That's the same as asking, "Have I begun my journey to my personal best?" If you can answer yes to that, then you not only look okay, you look fabulous!

YOUR WARDROBE

Marion

Standing in her closet for the third morning that week, Marion experienced a familiar frustration: a closet overflowing with clothes and absolutely nothing to wear. She stood in her pantyhose, looking around in despair. Her throat tightened and her pulse raced. As she realized she was once again running late, her frustration was compounded by what she saw as the hopelessness of it all. "How could I have spent so much money on clothes and still have nothing to wear?"

How often do you stare into your closet thinking the same thing? For many people, the answer is, "Oh, every day."

Open your closet. Take a look inside. Can you see everything you own? Can you easily select an outfit for work tomorrow? A Saturday night out? Cocktails with friends? Or do your clothes tell the story of your life from high school until today?

"Clothes make the man. Naked people have little or no influence in society."

—Mark Twain, American author and humorist

Your wardrobe is an essential tool on your journey. It protects you, it announces you, it defines your place in the world. All this from a bunch of fabric and a few belts and scarves? You bet. When you carefully select your wardrobe and thoughtfully design your look, you propel yourself further along on your journey…to a brand new level, a brand new you.

The Closet Cleanse

If you're like most people, organizing and updating the contents of your closet—a process I call the *Closet Cleanse*—isn't high on your list of favorite ways to spend a Saturday afternoon (and things are going to get pretty messy before they get organized). Nevertheless, this process offers great value on your journey.

19

Get ready...

It will—

- clear space and time in your life
- help to align your wardrobe with your desired image of yourself
- enable you to make charitable donations of unwanted, unworn clothes and thus benefit the less fortunate
- move you along on your path to your best self

Get set...

Set aside a morning or an afternoon. Clear enough space in your bedroom to create three piles of clothes.

Next, go to your closet. Look at every single piece of clothing and accessory. Sort them into three piles—

1. Haven't worn in two years or more
2. Wear occasionally
3. Absolutely love, wear it all the time

Go!!!

Pile #1 - Haven't worn in two years or more

This is the "immediate discard or donate" pile and into it should fall all items that evoke the same thought: "I never wear this, but I *should* keep it because...

...it cost a lot of money."

...I got it on sale."

...it was a gift."

...maybe I'll give it as a gift."

...I'll fit into that size again when I lose weight."

...I may need that size if I gain weight."

...the color is beautiful (even though it looks awful on me)."

...it reminds me of the time I..."

...I'm saving it for a special occasion."

If you haven't worn something in two years or more, chances are very good that all it's doing is taking up space in your life.

Despite every possible rationale (I've heard the ones listed above, as well as many others!), whatever the article of clothing, you're not wearing it for one reason only: it doesn't fit your life today.

Bottom line: The best thing—the only thing—to do is get rid of it. Give yourself permission to clear your life, and remember that your discards will be someone else's treasures. Contact a favorite charity or shelter and donate these items. You will be doing good for others while doing well for yourself.

Pile #2 - Wear occasionally

If the occasion is regular and recurring, such as the annual Caribbean Festival dinner, family reunion, or opera opening, it can stay. If it's an over-stretched navy sweater that tempts you when you're not feeling great or can't find anything else to wear, it goes into Pile #1 (and out the door!).

There are, of course, pieces like your black stretch jeans and oversized denim shirt that you wear only around the house or to run to the grocery store. If you feel good in them and they have a distinct purpose, they can stay.

Bottom line: So long as you wouldn't want to kill yourself if your photograph appeared on the front page of the local paper wearing them, they're keepers.

Otherwise—out with them!

Pile #3 - Absolutely love, wear it all the time

These are what I call your magic outfits: timeless, classic, or current trend pieces that call to you. They talk to you, boosting your confidence and power. They let you walk out the door into the world and say, "Here I am world. I'm ready for anything!"

Bottom line: This is your "keep" pile...*as long as* the outfit is truly a magic outfit, not something you wear all the time because it's comfortable or because it lets you fade into the woodwork. *Magic outfits* make you feel outstanding, chic, powerful...ready to face the world.

Now, the really hard part

Next, open your *Me File* and review your *Picture Me* activity, comparing the images you've selected to depict the person you want to become with the clothes you've decided to keep. How closely aligned are they?

I guarantee there will still be some hangers-on, things you're keeping that reflect where you've been, instead of where you want to go. Discarding these is the final step in clearing space in your closet...and your life.

Bottom line: These outfits and accessories go into Pile #1. One note, however: you may decide to give yourself permission to keep one or two of these outfits to help you through the transition. It may by a particular suit or a favorite belt or handbag. Keep them as a safety in the back of your closet. Reach for them, if you must.

Immediately—within the next 24 hours—pack your Pile #1 items into shopping bags, put them in the back seat of your car, and take them to the nearest donation location. Otherwise, the temptation to go back and retrieve items will undermine all the good you've just done. Remember, when you give these items to someone less fortunate, you actually give them a truly loving new home.

Marion's Closet Cleanse

Marion and I entered her closet like two soldiers venturing into battle. We locked the bedroom door. No one would enter or exit until our job was done. Every item in her closet came out onto the bed, the chairs, the floor—no flat surface was spared.

We determined the fate of the contents of her closet...piece by piece.

After four hours, a lot of laughing and even some tears, Marion was amazed to actually see space between the clothes hanging in her closet. "It looks like a wind chime," she said. "There's space for air and light between each item." She donated four huge boxes of clothes and 33 pair of shoes to her favorite charity.

Freeing space in your closet is freeing space in your life. Marion's mind, like her closet, was free, open, and clear. For the first time in many years, there was room for pleasing thoughts and feelings. A weight had been lifted from her closet, her shoulders, her life.

She could now begin the process of buying new pieces that matched the images of her best self as reflected in her *Picture Me* activity. Her new clothes and accessories would enable her to feel consistently fabulous and on the road to actualizing her best self, the one whose every outfit is a *magic outfit*.

YOUR ROUTINE

When your closet—and your mind—are clear, you can see everything you own and mix and match the pieces that work best for you. This is essential for establishing a simple and effective morning routine.

So you get out of bed, shower and venture into your whistle-clean closet. Still, you feel the pressure: you've got to live and work in these clothes for the rest of the day. Will they be appropriate from morning til night? Will you be comfortable all day, or begin to tug at a too-tight waistband or sneak your feet out of those heels by 9:30 a.m.?

"Owning too many [clothes] confuses me and I find I end up wearing the same wisely chosen outfits over and over again."

—*Elsa Klensch, TV host, syndicated columnist, and author*

I personally think in terms of uniforms. Not uniforms in the military sense, rather uniforms of clothing that work for me—the work me, the family me, the weekend me, the traveling me, the social me. I've found that this approach streamlines the process of dressing and is guaranteed to work for me every time.

To create these uniforms, I start with columns of color. Columns create the illusion of height (I'm 5'5" and every vertical inch helps!). A column of

23

color may otherwise be known as monochromatic dressing. A navy blue top paired with navy slacks and shoes or a taupe blouse, skirt, hose, and shoes. One continuous line of color that easily enables the eye to travel upward toward your most important feature, your face. Matched suits allow for this same ease and impact.

I have black, gray, and navy slacks, skirts, and tops that can be mixed and matched and a variety of colored jackets that can easily go over anything. Nearly everything in my closet matches everything else. *And I never buy more than I can comfortably fit in my closet...allowing for some breathing space between garments.*

What to Buy? Here are some guidelines for selecting pieces that will work for you all day, every day, without recreating the clutter you just worked so hard to eliminate.

Look for—

- Ways to accessorize or update the pieces you already have in your closet before buying anything new. (A simple change such as new buttons or a different belt can give a piece a brand new look.)

- Basic pieces that will mix and match easily (cotton or silk T-shirts and button downs, lightweight turtle-, crew, or V-neck sweaters, light weight wool trousers, skirts, and jackets). Lightweight fabrics are season-spanning and give you ultimate flexibility without clutter!

- Pieces in neutral colors that mix and match well with each other.

- Solids instead of patterns. (Solids never become outdated and they offer great flexibility for dressing up or dressing down.)

- Natural fabrics or natural fabric blends such as wool, cotton, and silk. (These wear well, clean easily, and feel comfortable.)

- Colorful current shirts, tops, and accessories to keep your basic pieces up-to-date.

Darlene

Single, accomplished, and looking for more, Darlene decided to give up her glamorous, jet-setting lifestyle, stop waiting for "Mr. Right," and adopt a baby. At the time, she was 46 years old.

Darlene adjusted every aspect of her life to this new, most important role. Sharp objects were hidden in drawers with childproof locks, hard edges on furniture were covered with soft bumpers, outlets made inaccessible by little plastic plugs. As a single parent, Darlene had no time for herself. So out went the sexy, diva-esque wardrobe. What would she need with that little black dress and double-breasted jacket completely covered in midnight blue sequins? Moms have no use for such things, she thought.

When I met Darlene, her daughter Charlotte was seven months old.

She told me about the day, a few weeks earlier, when she awoke to find that she had plenty of "Mommy clothes," but absolutely nothing to wear at "grown up" get-togethers. With the holiday season quickly approaching, Darlene started to panic. She was terrified to leave the house wearing yet another pair of prestained sweatpants. She realized that in the last year she had purchased all kinds of things for the house and for Charlotte, but nothing for herself.

I met Darlene at her house and we quickly emptied her closet of, oh, everything. Next, a shopping trip: Darlene had an envelope filled with coupons and gift certificates from a variety of department stores. Three and a half hours later, we left the stores with shopping bags of clothes that fit and flattered her. Her new wardrobe would make her look and feel fabulous and, as she informed me somewhere between the designer department and shoes, would allow her to be a grown-up single woman, not a Mom or a jet-setting single diva, on her first date since Charlotte's adoption.

The date was a disaster she later told me, but she looked and felt so great that she stopped on the way home to visit an old friend at a local bar. He introduced her to another friend who she's been dating for a year now.

Darlene and I review her wardrobe every six months, add pieces here and there, and recombine looks with the new seasonal touches, to make sure that she feels as great every time she walks out of the house as she did that first evening.

Shopping Strategies Shop only when you are equipped with positive energy, body-flattering undergarments, appropriate shoes and water to keep you refreshed. Even the most perfect outfit will look horrible with sweat socks and sneakers. And, if you're hungry or tired, nothing will look right.

Rule #1: When it comes to clothing, more isn't better, it's just more. Always look for quality over quantity.

Rule #2: You deserve a beautiful wardrobe *today*, no matter what milestone you've reached—or haven't reached—on your journey to your personal best. Shop for the body you have *right now*, not the size you used to be or hope to be one day, but now. (Besides, the body you'll have in six months will deserve something new!)

Some suggestions for saving time and money—
- Shop during retail store sales (especially end-of-season sales) and sample sales.
- Try discount stores, outlets, and resale shops for fabulous values.
- Find opportunities to trade with friends and relatives.
- If you're petite, visit the Junior Department for smaller sizes...and price tags to match!
- Develop a relationship with a salesperson or personal shopper who can be on the lookout for the styles, sizes, and price ranges you request.
- Remember: you'll get the greatest use and value out of the classic pieces you'll wear many times, styles that just never fall out of fashion: jackets, trousers, button down shirts, silk T's, BUT...
- Be sure to allow yourself one or two fashion pieces each year to update your classic wardrobe and have some fun!

26

More Strategies for Simplifying Your Routine

- Organize! Hang all skirts, all blouses, all slacks, and all jackets together or hang outfits together like suits or slacks with shirts and jackets that match. This makes the selection process very simple. Reach out and grab something—you can't go wrong!

- Find a terrific alterationist, tailor, or seamstress to keep your look polished and sharply tailored to your physique. Check the hems, seams, and pockets on all garments. Have any repairs done immediately.

- Have all your shoes resoled, waterproofed, and groomed. Having them ready at all times will give you more options each time you put together your look for the day.

- Make sure you have the proper undergarments for each outfit. For men this may mean a V-neck T-shirt under an open collar in place of that crewneck. Women should not wear a black bra under a white or other light-hued shirt or blouse. Match your undergarments to your skin tone for the greatest wearability.

When you eliminate clutter and develop a routine that works for you, you free up precious time and energy to focus on your day, your tasks, your audience, and your journey.

YOUR COLORS

Has anyone ever asked whether you've "had your colors done?" Perhaps it sounded strange. What on earth are they talking about? *My* colors? Yes, yours. Each of us has a color palette that complements our skin and hair color and enhances our natural style and personality. When we wear these colors, we naturally look (and feel!) brighter, even healthier, while other colors make us look (and feel!) "washed out" or "ill."

So, if you have heard a friend proclaim, "I'm a Spring," realize she doesn't mean that she pops up and down. She means that she was told that colors such as grass-green and peachy-peach look well on her and flatter her natural color characteristics.

Color is a powerful form of nonverbal communication that plays a huge role in our lives. Color makes us feel things and see things, and it influences how others respond to us. It announces us and our moods. It even evokes specific responses and reactions from those around us.

"The excitement at looking at a pair of red lips is inborn."

—Carlton Wagner, Director, The Wagner Institute for Color Research and author

We are naturally drawn to the colors that make us look and feel vibrant. After cleansing your closet, take a look inside, and you will see shades and inklings of your natural color palette.

Based in Science

For years, psychologists have studied the effects of color on the human mind and found that reds are energizing and attention-grabbing. Blues and greens are calming and soothing, very good to aid in communication. Yellow and orange are cheery and light-hearted. Soft pinks and pastels are often associated with romance and sweetness, children and springtime.

Bright and light colors make things appear larger while dark colors create a smaller impression. Neutral colors—traditionally beiges, grays, blacks, and navy blues—are easy to look at for long periods of time and are both soothing and powerful. Today, neutrals have come to include taupes, dark greens, shades of eggplant, and many blues. Mixing neutrals with other stronger colors is often a great way to create a memorable impression. Overall, effective use of color is an extraordinary, yet often overlooked aid in developing your personal message.

Your Appearance

The original color analysis process uses the imagery of the four seasons because the seasons are a natural event that provides simple, logical groupings of all the colors in the spectrum. It's easy to associate certain colors to each season...pumpkin in autumn, deep reds in winter, bright green in spring, and hazy blues in summer.

In their book, *Color Me Beautiful—Looking Your Best* (Madison Books, 1995), Mary Spillane and Christine Sherlock explain, "Most of us have always felt some colors suited us rather better than others, but it was all a matter of experimentation, trial and error. The Seasonal Color Palette had a sense of logic...Millions of women who've adopted the system can confirm that it is not limiting but liberating."

Carla

Carla came to me with a shock of silver gray hair that crossed her forehead. The orange-red hair on the rest of her head was styled in a chin-length bob. She was wearing a mustard-colored shirt, turquoise jewelry and black slacks. She introduced herself and good-naturedly told me that she loved color but that people often asked whether she was feeling all right. "Why do people react that way to me?" she wondered aloud.

Apart from the color blitz people experienced when Carla entered a room, she had chosen a palette that didn't flatter her hair and skin tone. Her skin was very pink. Her silver-gray hair looked yellow next to the orange-red color of the rest of her head. And rather than bright, warm, and healthy, her mustard colored shirts and jackets made her look drawn and sickly.

Step one was to cover Carla's hair and put on a white blouse. The absence of color allowed us to experiment freely without distraction. Using over 150 dinner-napkin size pieces of colored fabrics, we began the color analysis process. We chose colors that were blue-based such as dusty rose, as well as yellow-based such as orange. We draped Carla in entire families of color including blues, greens, green-blues, and blue-greens. Within an hour, Carla saw herself in every shade of color in the spectrum and immediately noticed the difference.

When the drapes of color had any amount of yellow in them, Carla began to see shadows and dullness in her skin and eyes. When we placed colors like silver and cherry-red near her skin, Carla came alive. Her face brightened, her eyes sparkled, she looked as if she had applied a light layer of lipstick and blush and she started to smile. "Wow! What a difference!" was all she could say. "Do more."

On Your Own To find a Color Consultant in your area, contact The Association of Image Consultants International at www.aici.org or call toll-free (877) 247-3319.

I have been color analyzed many times and found each time to be a highly worthwhile investment. However, should you choose to venture out on your own to find your own best palette, *Color Me Beautiful—Looking Your Best* is filled with ultra-practical ideas and strategies for identifying your color palette and making it work for you.

Or, like Carla, you can simply experiment with different colors next to your skin and hair to identify the colors that flatter you and make you look healthy, rested, and vibrant.

If you've gone through the *Closet Cleanse*, you've afforded yourself a valuable shortcut: visit your closet and take out your magic outfits. Stand in front of a mirror, and in good lighting, hold these up to your face. Since these are the outfits that make you feel healthy and vibrant, chances are that these are also colors that work well with your natural palette.

By the way, what's true for clothes is also true for make-up. (There's a reason that pink lipstick never looked quite right on you!)

When your clothes and make-up complement your natural color characteristics and your personality, you've found your best colors...and an important part of yourself.

YOUR MAKE-UP

While every element of your appearance sends messages to the rest of the world, nothing communicates faster or more directly than your face. Your face serves as your communications center. It is often the first thing people see, sometimes the only thing they see, and always the part of your physical self on which their eyes linger longest. Eyes are particularly important, indicating character, depth, and focus in a single glance. Intrigued and mystified by the power of the eyes, 18th century poets often referred to them as "the window to the soul."

"Even I don't wake up looking like Cindy Crawford."

—*Cindy Crawford, supermodel and entrepreneur*

That face of yours is a work of art. It is a precious, one-of-a-kind oil painting by a master painter. Imagine this painting on its own, and then, in your mind, surround it with a beautiful, delicate frame. This frame is your make-up, the finishing touch that accentuates your favorite features and subdues those you may like less.

For most of us, approaching a department store make-up counter is an act of bravery. We may advance and retreat a few times and decline offers of help ("Help? Me? Oh, no thanks, I'm just looking."). Eventually, we conquer the dread and the fear of being thoroughly overwhelmed by the sheer number of choices and colors, not to mention the fear of spending large sums of money on products that look great on the woman behind the counter, but not on us.

We take the plunge.

But it's an expensive hit-or-miss proposition that can quickly add sizeable clutter to our drawers...and our lives. (I for one will admit to having sampled so many different lipsticks, eye shadows, and foundations that a day came when I could no longer open or close the drawers in my bathroom cabinet.)

Make-up Counter Confidence

Here are some pointers to help with your next close encounter at the make-up counter:

Foundation must match your skin color and tone. The closer the match, the better. If your skin is oily, look for an oil-free foundation. If your skin is dry, look for a light cream foundation.

Foundation provides protection against the elements and often has added benefits like moisturizer and UV protection that help keep your skin young and healthy.

Mascara opens and brightens your eyes. If you have fair or light hair and lashes, ask to see samples of gray or light brown mascara. If your hair is dark, look for dark brown or black.

Blush should give your face a natural glow, not show up as a bright streak across your cheek. Ask to try on a powder or cream blush in a shade that complements your skin tone: peachy to suntan or pink to deep rose.

Using a fluffy brush to apply powder blush gives you a more natural result…less of a streak, more of an even glow. (The tiny brushes that come in the packages are strictly for show. Invest in a good blush brush. It's worth it!)

Lipstick is the finishing touch. Find a lipstick color that is one or two shades darker than your natural lip color. This will simply add more distinction to your lip line without becoming a center of attention.

Optional: A light finishing powder will blend the colors on your face and create a natural look. Apply a small amount with a clean fluffy brush. (Try this just once to see the difference it makes!)

Make the Time

Even the most well-chosen make-up doesn't accomplish anything sitting in your drawer or make-up case. So, the next step is to schedule time to apply it in the morning.

Now, if you're like the millions of women trying to do too much, applying make-up is probably number nine or ten on your list of morning To-Dos. And if you're at all unsure about how best to apply make-up, it probably won't make the list at all.

So here's a useful rule of thumb: establish a make-up practice you can comfortably follow every day. Consider: 1.) how much time you can realistically allot, 2.) the look you prefer for day versus evening, and 3.) whether you will take time to "touch up" during the course of the day. And persist! Like anything else, it will take time to integrate this new practice into your daily routine.

For a simple five-minute routine, apply make-up in this order: foundation, mascara, blush, and lipstick.

YOUR HAIR

According to Colin Lively, the Hair and Color Director at the Elizabeth Arden Red Door Salon in New York City, both women and men make two common mistakes with their hair. "They get trapped in an outdated style letting 'outdated' become their message," he explains, adding, "They also try hair colors that look artificial. These aren't flattering…they're artificial. People, fashions, and lives change, and hair must change too. Up-to-date styles and natural colors always work."

"How you look tells the world how you feel."

—*Sergio Valenti, fashion designer*

What about you? When was the last time you updated your hairstyle? Are you having a bad hair day? Are you having a bad hair year? Don't pull it back or stuff it under a hat and ignore it. Fix it! Once and for all, get a fabulous haircut, a style you love, and one that works in your life. Change your hair color to flatter and brighten your entire face.

Begin to notice hairstyles. When you see a style you like, ask the person for the name and phone number of the stylist. Don't be shy. The person will be flattered and the stylist will be thrilled.

The best stylists have a talent for identifying the most flattering and manageable hairstyle for each individual client. Once you find a stylist you'd like to try, bring photos and ask questions. If you're considering a radical change, you may choose to take it in stages or just go for it. Hair is one of the easiest things to change and the change can influence your day, your year, or your life in a big way.

Stephen

Stephen was a 51-year-old CEO who felt he needed to look younger once he began to lose his hair. He had taken to using "the swoop" or the "comb-over" to camouflage his thinning locks, a questionable strategy that always seems to put years on someone's face.

Yet, Stephen had a sweet, young face. We discussed the possibility of a new hairstyle. He resisted the idea at first, but, when I asked him if he really believed that no one noticed his hair flopping in the wind when he was running late for a meeting, he smiled and agreed to give it a try.

After just minutes in the stylist's chair, Stephen looked years younger. The long gray strands were gone, and he discovered that his own hair had more growth than he realized. Without exception, everyone who saw Stephen told him how terrific he looked. Stephen's eyes grew brighter, his smile grew broader, his face relaxed (from all the smiling) and his message was clear: he looked great and he felt great. The great feeling was further reinforced by all the compliments he was receiving. And nothing supports your decisions better than positive public opinion.

YOUR HYGIENE

We recognize odor and fragrance even before we register a person's visual image. While odor and fragrance may be related, they are not equal.

Let's begin with fragrance.

Fragrance should be light and it should travel with you...not before you or after you. If your fragrance—cologne, perfume, lotion, or aftershave—announces your arrival or lingers after you're gone, you may need to rethink it.

Strong fragrance can be so distracting that formal choirs and orchestras prohibit the wearing of fragrance during rehearsals and performances. It's been known to sabotage performances and careers by causing sneezing, watery eyes, and troubled breathing.

"Hygiene is two thirds of health."

—Lebanese Proverb

Fragrance is an enhancer, the ribbon on an otherwise well-turned-out package. Avoid making fragrance the whole story...or the topic of conversation after you leave.

And, remember that despite its origins as a means of masking body odor, fragrance is not intended to replace proper and appropriate personal hygiene practices such as daily bathing and oral hygiene.

As for odor, perspiration can cause clothing to have an unpleasant odor. Any garment that sits directly on your skin such as underwear, T-shirts, socks or hosiery will absorb the greatest amount of perspiration and should be laundered after each wearing. Garments such as suits, jackets, trousers, or skirts that sit farther from your skin or have a layer of foundation between them and your skin may be cleaned less frequently.

Saving Strategies Protect your garments and yourself from unnecessary chemicals and save on dry cleaning bills by spot-cleaning soiled items before taking the whole garment to the dry cleaner.

Give your clothes an "air shower" by hanging garments on separate hangers outside in the fresh air or near a window or a fan. (My grandmother always said, "Nothing cures better than fresh air and sunshine.") If, after 24 to 48 hours, the wrinkles and odors have not disappeared, consider dry cleaning. Most wool or wool-blend fabrics require very little cleaning and will do quite nicely in the fresh air, if given the opportunity.

START TODAY!

1. Go to your closet. Take out five garments that you haven't worn in two or more years.
2. Go to your make up or toiletries drawer. Pick out five items you've never used such as lipsticks or powders, colognes or shampoos that you received as a gift-with-purchase or as samples.
3. Select three pair of shoes that were bought to complete specific outfits that you discarded years ago.
4. Go to your closet or your father's, husband's, son's, boyfriend's or significant other's closet. Pick out five ties that have not been worn in two years or more.
5. Run—don't walk!—with all these items to the nearest local charity or shelter and donate them within the next 24 hours to people who will use and appreciate them.

FOR MORE INSPIRATION, DISCOVERY, AND IDEAS

- ***Color with Style*** by Donna Fujii, Graphic-Sha, 1992
- ***Color Me Beautiful—Looking your Best*** by Mary Spillane and Christine Sherlock, Madison Books, 1995
- ***It's A Fit*** by Susan Graver, QVC Publishing, Inc., 2000
- ***40 Over 40*** by Brenda Kinsel, Wildcat Canyon Press, 1999

Your Appearance

- *Plus Style* by Suzan Nanfeldt, Penguin Books, 1996
- *Dressing the Whole Person: Nine Ways to Create Harmony and Balance in Your Wardrobe (and Prosperity in Your Life)* by Evana Maggiore, Mansion Publishing LTD, 1998
- *Formulas for Dressing the Whole Person* by Evana Maggiore and Louise Elerding, Mansion Publishing LTD, 2000
- *Fashion Secrets Mother Never Taught You* by Ginger Burr, Total Image Consultants, 1999
- *The Indispensable Guide to Classic Men's Clothing* by Josh Karlen and Christopher Sulavik, Tatra Press, 1999
- *A Gentleman's Guide to Appearance* by Clinton T. Greenleaf III, Adams Media Corp., 2000
- *Dress Casually for Success* by Mark Weber and The Van Heusen Creative Design Group, McGraw-Hill, 1997

3
Your Physical Health

Your body is the vehicle that will carry you throughout your journey to your best self. Its health, strength, and vitality shape your image and directly impact how *you* see and feel about yourself and how *the world* sees and feels about you.

> *"You have to stay in shape. My grandmother started walking five miles a day when she was 60. She's 97 today and we don't know where the hell she is."*
>
> —*Ellen Degeneres, actress, comedian*

The saying, "When you have your health, you have everything," may sound trite, yet health and vitality are prerequisite to arriving at your personal best in style. You can't get from here to there in a rundown Chevy with flat tires. (Okay, maybe you can, but it will take a whole lot longer, and won't be nearly as much fun!)

All of this means your body deserves the same level of respect and TLC you'd give to a shiny new, gleaming red Ferrari. Yet studies show that in the daily tug and pull of life, health isn't often a priority.

Carl

Meet Carl, a senior manager at an international pharmaceutical company. Carl came to me looking for help with his image and immediately began venting his frustrations over his low energy level and diminished appearance. "Before this merger started, I lost 45 pounds and was feeling terrific," he said. "I was working out every day and watching what I ate.

I had energy to spare, and I was leaving work at a reasonable hour. Now it's three months later. I drink Coke all day just to stay awake. I'm so tired, I've gained back 25 pounds, and I'm sluggish and hungry all the time. The stress may just kill me."

Stress and strain—physical or emotional—have a way of forcing us back into old patterns and unhealthy habits. Naturally, there seem to be endless varieties of stressful stimuli that come our way in life:

- small children at home
- a tight budget
- a move out of a home or into a new one
- the start or end of a relationship
- the start or end of a job
- the opening or closing of a business
- marriage or divorce
- an unexpected large expense

Health and nutrition are often the first casualties. "I can't worry about what I'm eating! I've got to move out of my house by next Thursday, and I haven't even started packing!" The pressure's on. We simply want to get to the other side of events or circumstances that are vexing us. We indulge in comfort food, eat on the run or snack late at night. We skip workouts or neglect exercise altogether. Sleep is interrupted by fears about what the future will hold or thoughts about what we didn't finish today and what we have to do tomorrow.

Of course, stress isn't the only factor that compromises physical health. Inertia in the form of unhealthful habits that are tough to break is a tremendous contributor. Doritos, Pepsi, Milky Ways, and Krispy Kremes call to us, tempting us with textures, flavors, smart packaging, and insistent advertising.

We indulge, often triggered by certain moments in the day (the mid-morning munchies, the 3:00 p.m. slump, the Wednesday night favorite TV program). Changing these patterns through discipline and avoidance of these triggers is a tough job, especially once poor habits have gotten a firm foothold in our lives.

All-or-nothing thinking is yet another culprit. Many of us take a "110 percent" or a "minus 10 percent" approach to exercise and good nutrition ("If I can't work out every day, I won't bother going for a walk a few times a week" or "I may as well have the lasagna and ice cream for dinner, after all I did eat those Doritos at lunch").

As if all this weren't enough, too many treats and/or lack of physical activity may make us sluggish and tired, but they don't otherwise have an immediate harmful effect on our health and vitality. We can survive with these foods in our diets; we can manage without regular exercise. Maybe we won't feel great, but we won't be incapacitated either. There's no immediate price to pay. In today's point-and-click world, we are used to immediate cause and effect. Since the effect of poor health habits may not be felt for years, we think: "I'll worry about it tomorrow"...a tomorrow that never comes.

We view diet and exercise as forms of *discipline*, with all the negative connotations that can accompany that word. What about *joie de vivre*? Who wants to live life on a never-ending "diet"?

In reality, the best health strategies and regimens don't feel like discipline because they fit neatly into your life and allow for some flexibility. The occasional indulgence in an otherwise healthy lifestyle is all the more enjoyable because it isn't accompanied by overwhelming feelings of guilt and self-abandonment.

Here are some tips for mastering the elusive goal of good health and nutrition as you take this most important step forward on your journey to your personal best. (Let's rev-up that Ferrari!)

YOUR FAMILY HEALTH HISTORY AND YOUR HABITS

Open your *Me File*. Find a fresh new page and take some quiet time to answer these questions:

> *"Everyone is kneaded out of the same dough but not baked in the same oven."*
>
> —*Yiddish Proverb*

Your Family Health History
- Do you have a clear idea of your family's health history?
- Are you aware of the existence of heart disease, diabetes and other chronic health problems in your bloodline one or two generations back?
- How long have people in your family lived, on average?

Your Medical Record
- When was your last complete physical?
- Do you know your cholesterol count and your current and optimal blood pressure?
- Have you had a cardiac stress test recently?
- If you're a woman over 40, do you get regular mammograms and Pap smears?
- If you're a man over 50, do you have your PSA level checked each year to screen for prostate problems?

Your Habits
- Do you eat a balanced diet of lean proteins and grains and plenty of fresh fruits and vegetables?
- Do you often skip meals?
- Do you exercise regularly?
- Do you smoke?
- Do you drink alcohol on a frequent basis (more than 2-3 times/week)?
- Do you have a high stress job or lifestyle?
- Are you completely exhausted by the end of your work day?
- Can you climb one flight of stairs (approximately 22 steps) without getting winded?
- Can you do at least three sit-ups?
- Do you often complain of back pain?

YOUR FITNESS AND NUTRITION

According to Adin Alai, a sports medicine specialist and an American Fitness Professionals and Associates (AFPA) certified nutritional consultant and personal trainer, there are simple steps we can all take to improve our eating and exercise habits.

Here's his list—

- Visit your physician for a complete physical once every year. Be certain to do this before undertaking any major changes to your current activity level.

- Exercise! Include some cardiovascular activity in your exercise routine. These are aerobic exercises that challenge and expand the capacity of your heart and lungs. They include swimming, walking briskly, jogging, and cycling. Also in this category of activity are exercises performed for a duration of 20 minutes or more on equipment such as a stationary bike, stair climber, or treadmill. In just one or two weeks, you will see and feel a difference in your physique and your energy level.

"Don't let life discourage you; everyone who got where he is had to begin where he was."

—*Richard L. Evans, Mormon elder, speaker, and author*

In addition to cardiovascular exercise, include some strength training or resistance exercises in your weekly routine. Resistance training prevents injuries and improves your appearance. There's also scientific evidence that it improves bone mass, a benefit of particular value to menopausal and post-menopausal women. Examples of resistance training are weight lifting, working on weight machines, or using resistance bands to challenge muscles and improve their strength and endurance. Also in this category of activity are exercises that strengthen your abdominal muscles such as sit-ups or crunches. These are essential for protecting your back muscles since they support your back throughout your daily activities.

Finally, stretch at both the start and the end of your workout. Begin your workout with some small, simple movements (marching in place, step touches, hamstring curls, easy lunges) to increase your heart rate slightly and get your blood flowing. Follow this with light stretches that concentrate on your lower back and hamstrings. After your workout, your muscles are warm and elastic, making a post-workout stretch essential for getting more length out of a muscle and improving its resilience. Since a flexible muscle is far less likely to pull or snap, flexibility prevents injuries. And, when it's combined with resistance training, a solid stretch routine also helps to improve your posture.

- Ease into any new activity to avoid injury and burnout, even if this means starting with a daily short walk around the block or using the stairs instead of taking the elevator. Begin slowly, build steadily and your progress over time will surprise you.

- Have fun! You must look forward to your chosen physical activity or you simply won't make the time to do it. So go for a bike ride on a beautiful Spring or Summer morning. Play with your children instead of watching them. Take a dance class or walk to the park. Tap into your own sense of enjoyment and get fit at the same time.

- Drink at least eight 8-ounce glasses of water each day. This will help to flush out the impurities that hold fat and toxins in your system. You'll also feel more awake and energetic…and may even lose a bit of that puffiness around the eyes!

- Reduce your intake of carbonated and caffeinated beverages. They cause dehydration and cravings for more of the same in your system.

- Eat more vegetables—all day, every day. Eat more fruit as well, but try to do so before midday. After noon, many people find fruits more difficult to digest. Citrus, berries, apple, and melon are energizing and refreshing.

- Eat three balanced meals and two fruit and/or vegetable snacks. This practice will discourage overeating in the latter parts of the day.

- Don't skip any meal, especially breakfast. Your body and brain need the early morning energy for optimum performance.

- Stay within five pounds of your ideal weight. (**Important!** Your ideal weight is that number where you feel your honest best...not what the standardized charts tell you!)

Select one or a few of these tips to jumpstart your fitness and nutrition goals.

Remember Carl, the senior manager in the throes of a merger? Carl began to take a hard look at his health habits and his nutrition. He had a physical for the first time in three years. He learned that he had a family history of heart disease. Motivated primarily by fear, he decided to cut out the Cokes in favor of water, eat more vegetables, and leave the office for 10 minutes each day—rain or shine—to walk outside.

Within one week, he began to feel the difference. He had more vitality and a far better outlook about the changes at work. Today, his staff often accompanies him on his walks and, occasionally, to the salad bar.

START TODAY!

- Find out about your family history, particularly a history of heart- or stress-related illness.
- Schedule a complete physical if you haven't had one in the last year.
- Begin to pay attention to what you eat and introduce more fruits and vegetables. (Vegetable drinks are delicious and satisfying!)
- Commit ten minutes a day to exercise!
- Start slow and persist. You will see a difference.

FOR MORE INSPIRATION, DISCOVERY, AND IDEAS

Visit www.AFPAfitness.com, the American Fitness Professionals and Associates website or www.RealAge.com. Both include links to articles and a great deal of other information by topic.

- *The Zone: A Dietary Road Map to Lose Weight Permanently: Reset Your Genetic Code: Prevent Disease: Achieve Maximum Physical Performance* by Barry Sears, HarperCollins, 1995
- *Sugar Busters!: Cut Sugar to Trim Fat* by H. Leighton Steward, Ballantine Books, 1998
- *Stretching* by Bob Anderson, Shelter Publications, 2000

Your Home

Home. Say the word a few times to yourself. It has a warm and soothing sound. Home is a place to lay your head, a safe haven, a space filled with people who love you, where you're surrounded by the items that hold special meaning for you.

Jenna and Steve

Jenna and Steve had lived in their small apartment for seven years. When they moved in, they each brought boxes and milk crates filled with stuff. After seven years, they had double and, in some cases, triple the stuff. The furniture remained exactly where they put it without much thought when they moved in. "Just for now," a phrase they uttered often during those first months of settling in to their new life together, became a full-time permanent approach to home décor.

Of course, they're not alone. So many of us treat our homes like a storage space—and not a very well-organized one at that. For Jenna and Steve, that meant boxes that had been unpacked and left in the same spot for so long that they became invisible.

> *"He is happiest, be he king or peasant, who finds peace in his home."*
>
> —*Johann von Goethe, philosopher, author*

In fact, their apartment was the very model of what I call the "Rule of Stuff": when you can't find what you're looking for, you go out and buy it again, even if you already own three. And, without a sense of where anything is, you tend to be rather nondiscriminating about all of it. You haven't the vaguest idea whether you need new coasters, making that trendy set of green bamboo coasters all the more tempting. "Just for now" becomes "What the heck?" as in "Let's just get them, we'll probably find a use for them during the holidays, what the heck?" And...you guessed it: yet more stuff suddenly appears.

Jenna, Steve, and I talked for a long time about their goals and their hopes for their home. "We visit friends and their homes look so pulled together," Steve complained, "I feel like we're still in college because our place looks like a dorm room."

Interesting...I thought. We talked more about their lifestyles and busy work schedules. With each of them working a minimum of a 55-hour week ("Sometimes we actually have dinner together," said Steve), neither had an organized way of making the time to arrange their things, purge extra stuff, and plan a home style that matched their lifestyle and personal aesthetics, which, explained Jenna, oddly enough, tended toward clean lines and simple pieces. In addition, a beloved library of collectible books remained half-stored in boxes, half-strewn around the apartment in various hiding places.

We talked for hours. Then, realization dawned. "You know what this place looks like, Lauren?" said Jenna, "It looks like I feel."

Bingo!

Your home is a great example of your image in action. For better or for worse, it will reflect your image of yourself in your mind's mirror, the point you've reached on your journey.

The very good news is that once you begin the external change, you move further along on the internal part of the journey to your personal best.

YOUR SPACE

Without question, a well-organized home that reflects your personal style supports you on your journey. Like your magic outfits, your home should make you feel fabulous and reflect your desired image. All the things in your home should be things you love and love to use. Understandably, they should be accessible so they can fulfill their potential to enhance your life daily.

As a result of the daily demands on our time and energy and because we see, according to one study, up to 7,000 advertising images daily, we shop and we buy, shop and buy, shop and buy.

This is one key reason the clutter battle is endless.

Yet, having many things that have no meaning doesn't enhance your sense of well-being. Like your wardrobe, more things in your home aren't better. They're just more. And the more you have, the more you have to put away, dust, insure, replace, repair...the list goes on.

Fortunately, the principles of the *Closet Cleanse* easily adapt to the *Home Cleanse*, an activity that will save your entire home from being consumed by clutter.

The Home Cleanse As in the case of the *Closet Cleanse*, be prepared for things to get messy before they get organized, but this process as well offers great value on your journey.

Get ready...
It will—
- clear space and time in your life to focus on reaching your personal best
- help to align your home with your desired image of yourself
- enable you to make charitable donations of unwanted, unused items and thus to benefit the less fortunate
- move you along on your path to your best self

Get set...
Realize that there's only so much you can do in one day. Give yourself time and space to achieve small changes over time. The *Home Cleanse* is a

process of weeks or months. Trying to finish in a shorter timeframe is a recipe for frustration and burnout. You'll end up abandoning your quest, tired and exasperated (I know...I tried!).

Work room by room, starting with a specific closet or cabinet in each room. Designate a start and end time as well. By beginning small and defining a limited space and time, you increase the chances of seeing your effort through from start to finish. Seeing your progress from space to space will help to propel you forward. If you jump from the bathroom cabinet to the bedroom drawers, then to the kitchen, you will neither see nor feel the sense of accomplishment needed to persevere.

Many clients have found the kitchen and the bedroom closet their toughest to conquer alone. Therefore, when attempting this on your own, I recommend starting in a bathroom or a guest closet or your living room. The process will become easier as you grow more comfortable making fast decisions and sticking with them. By the time you get to the tough stuff, you'll wonder why you didn't do this years ago.

Clear enough space in each room to create three piles—
1. Immediately discard or donate
2. Maybe, maybe not
3. Absolutely love/need it

Go!!!
Pile #1 - Immediately discard or donate

Into this pile go—
1. Things you haven't used or can't imagine using in the next 12 months:
   - the wedding gifts still in their original packages
   - items with no specific use or purpose

2. What I call your "best intentions" stuff:
   - anything you've been holding onto to use "some day"
   - anything you've been holding onto "just for now"
   - anything that's broken that you've intended to fix "one day" for the last two years or more

In the next 24 hours, donate what you can to your favorite charities, schools, or homes for the less fortunate. For anything that remains, get a jumbo-sized garbage bag and bid these items farewell.

Pile #2
Maybe, maybe not

In this pile we have—
- The fondue pot you bought for your first wedding anniversary, but haven't seen since. Keep it if you feel an oncoming urge for bread and warm cheese (or fruit and chocolate!), but be sure it's visible. Remember the old adage: "Out of sight, out of mind."

- The cake plate with the birds plucking the fish out of the water. Clearly, it would not have been your first choice, but Aunt Sally so enjoyed giving it to you. Keep it for when Aunt Sally comes to visit, but store it out of the way until then. Just remember where you stored it.

Pile #3
Absolutely love/need it

Into this pile go—
- The few well-chosen things that reflect your personal style, give you a sense of joy, and simply enhance every moment you spend in your home. Put them where you can see and access them at all times.

Jenna and Steve followed this process in a disciplined fashion one room at a time, one box or cabinet at a time, one item at a time.

Each time they opened a cabinet or a box, they made an on-the-spot decision about the item(s) by asking simple questions to determine which of their three piles the item should fall into—
- Do we love this? Does it hold special memories or some other importance for us in our lives today? If it met these criteria, it stayed.
- Do we need this? Do we use it frequently or regularly (each day, week or month)? Does it have some special utility in our lives today?

Here, in their own words, are the rules they followed—

"We cleaned out one box or cabinet each week, without fail."

"If we hadn't used it in the last 12 months and/or didn't see an opportunity to use it in the next 12 months, out it went."

"Everything broken or outdated—like the decanter with the missing top or the microwave from Jenna's college dorm room that took 15 minutes to melt a piece of cheese—went."

"Every item we decided to keep was put in an accessible place where it could be found, used, and enjoyed. Each item was placed in a spot based on its frequency of use and importance in our lives.

Jenna and Steve went through the process and kept only the things they absolutely loved and would use regularly. They even found the room to display and access their cherished library.

YOUR SURROUNDINGS

Your newly uncluttered space opens your life to events, people, and circumstances that propel you further along the path to your best self.

How will you adorn this newly available space in your life?

Start by looking at your magic outfits. What colors are they? These colors naturally attract you which makes them a helpful starting point for decorating your entire world.

Be adventurous! Many of us gravitate to the simplicity and flexibility of white. On walls, white tends to be stark and harsh on the eyes. And, whites don't create a relationship between your space and the things in your space. Colors in various shades and textures bring a room together (couch pillows that match that scrumptious burgundy in your living room rug, for instance) and are thus inviting and soothing. When a room works, you feel welcome in it.

Let colors work from room to room so that you and your guests don't feel like you're stepping from house to house—or planet to planet!—simply by walking from one room to another. Create a theme using your favorite beiges or burgundies to add to the pleasure you get from being in your surroundings.

"A beautiful home is no accident. It takes both inspiration and careful, thoughtful planning."

— *Lauren Smith and Rose Bennett Gilbert, interior designers, color consultants, and authors*

Think of yourself as dressing each room. Take a closer look at your navy and burgundy living room with the gray carpet, for instance. If it were a navy and burgundy suit, you might wear it with gray shoes. You might add a blouse in a shade of burgundy, navy or gray. That shade could be just the right color for your walls, or for one accent wall.

Then, you'd add earrings, a watch, and a bracelet in silver or gold. These accessories are the beautiful pieces and little accents that you can sprinkle around your room to add sparkle and excitement. Perhaps a mirror with a silver frame and the silver candlesticks (the wedding gift that you finally unpacked) on the mantle. Or you might add a navy velvet pillow with silver braid trim on the sofa.

These small touches of your favorite accents add to the positive energy you feel in your space. When you surround yourself with your favorite things in colors that are flattering and fun for you, you carry over your image by design into the most important areas of your life.

Note: When your color scheme is "in" and readily available in the stores, buy all the coordinating pieces you love. Otherwise, you may not be able to find those special "add-on" pieces for a number of years, if at all.

Finally, invest wisely in major pieces of furniture such as a bedroom or dining room set. Shop around. Make lists of the features that appeal to you and those you prefer to avoid. Narrow your list down to a few favorites and visit those showrooms repeatedly. Sit on the couch. Lie down on the bed. Picture the pieces in your home. Eventually, your best choice will be clear. But most importantly: take your time! Do not be forced into a major purchase by an eager salesperson. Remember, you're the one who has to live with it!

START TODAY!

In your *Me File*:
- Write your answers to these questions:
    "How does my home feel?"
    "How do I want to feel in my home?"
- Cut and paste pictures and make notes about places you see that reflect the visual image of the home of your dreams.
- Open your storage closet. Pick three items you have never used. Take them to a local charity or shelter and donate them within the next 24 hours.
- List five steps you can take immediately to bring your home closer to the home of your dreams. Can you organize your closets, paint your walls or bookcases or reduce the clutter in your home office?
- Each week, review just one of these steps...and then do it!

FOR MORE INSPIRATION, DISCOVERY, AND IDEAS

Contact the National Association of Professional Organizers (NAPO) to find a professional organizer in your area at www.napo.net or (512) 206-0151.

- ***Christopher Lowell's Seven Layers of Design: Fearless, Fabulous Decorating*** by Christopher Lowell, Discovery Books, 2000
- ***Real Life Decorating*** by Linda Hallam, Better Homes and Gardens Books, 2000
- ***Debbie Travis' Weekend Projects: More than 55 One-of-a-Kind Designs You Can Make in Under Two Days*** by Debbie Travis and Barbara Dingle, Clarkson Potter, 2000

Your Relationships

YOUR PROPELLERS,
MAINTAINERS, AND DRAINERS

Propellers I remember standing on a wooden stool in my grandfather's pharmacy, barely tall enough to reach the cash register, as he showed me how to make change. "If someone gives you a dollar and the charge is $.60, which coins do they get in return?" he asked me. At five years old, I already knew the answer.

"The real test of friendship is: can you literally do nothing with the other person? Can you enjoy those moments of life that are utterly simple?"

—Eugene Kennedy, university professor, speaker, author

By the time I was 7, he paid me "one of each"—one penny, one nickel, one dime, and one quarter—41¢ for a day's work. In the years to come, I learned what it meant to be an independent businessowner as I watched my grandfather manage employee issues—interviewing, hiring, and firing, while helping customers who needed special services, care, or assistance.

I counted inventory, rearranged the products on the shelves, and refilled the candy stand. "These skills will come in handy for you no matter what you choose to do," he'd tell me. Our close relationship and everything I learned by watching him work propelled me into a life in business.

Image Matters!

I call these your Propellers...the people whose ideas, encouragement, and example moved you in some significant way toward the achievement of your dreams and ultimately your personal best. Propellers are a little like your magic outfits. They're there to make you strong. They inspire and support you. When you're with them, you feel anything is possible. With them your best qualities come shining through.

Maintainers Maintainers are your "Steady-Eddies," the solid, cool, strong people in your life who keep you from jumping off a cliff when you've forgotten to look down. They're the dependable black stretch jeans and the denim shirt in your wardrobe...you count on them, they're always there and ready.

Maintainers force you to view all the possibilities and options in your life. In their level-headed way, they won't let you rule out options or put all your eggs in one basket. They will also force you to be brutally honest with yourself. Amazingly, you will love them all the more for it.

Drainers In her book *The Artist's Way*, Julia Cameron describes people she calls "crazy makers." "Crazy makers" are individuals who've mastered the art of keeping you off balance and unsure of yourself, often with their eccentric energy and inability to focus on any pursuit, person, idea, or job for very long. She might well have been describing the people I call Drainers.

Drainers deplete the living energy from every ounce of your being. Drainers are like the expensive outfit that you feel compelled to wear because you paid one month's salary for it. Even though it will never fit right, give you comfort, or make you feel great.

Drainers hold you back, sometimes unwittingly, sometimes with intention. They undermine you by projecting their own insecurity or unhappiness onto you by saying things like, "Oh, you've lost eight pounds already! That's great, but be careful. You don't want to get too thin. Here, have an Oreo."

Nevertheless, Drainers do serve a positive purpose in life: they inspire a measure of doubt, and keep you from becoming complacent, in their own unique and often painful way. They cause you to question yourself, your ideas, and your plans. In so doing, Drainers tend to help your Maintainers keep you from running in 20 directions at once.

Record in your *Me File* the name of at least one Drainer in your life. Describe your relationship with this person. Describe how this relationship has served you and what it might have cost you.

We need all three... It's a law of the universe: into every life will fall a number of Propellers, Maintainers, and Drainers...thank goodness, because in reality, we need to be surrounded by all three.

57

Image Matters!

If our personal and professional circles included only Propellers, we'd be too exhausted from the energy and the pace to accomplish anything for ourselves.

A life filled only with Maintainers might be too complacent, relaxed, or downright boring.

Too many Drainers, and life would be so exhausting and discouraging that any dream would automatically become "the impossible dream."

Your journey to your personal best must include a healthy balance of these three types of people.

Take out your *Me File* and do a bit of Image Matters! accounting: add up the number of Propellers, Maintainers, and Drainers in your life.

How did you do? Is there a balance? What does your answer suggest about the types of people who are in your life? How much time do you spend with each? When do you feel happiest? When are you most productive? When are you your personal best? Record your answers in your *Me File*.

Once you examine this balance, here are some strategies for managing these essential relationships so they can support you through your journey:

Managing Propellers
- Bask in the faith and confidence these people have in you.
- Use their ideas and energy to expand your horizons. (Believe in yourself! Your Propellers certainly believe in you!)
- Keep them nearby and don't hesitate to call when you need an ego boost or a shoulder to lean on.

Managing Maintainers
- Check in regularly for a dose of reason and logic, especially if you're facing a difficult decision or situation along your journey.

- Appreciate their perspective and the balance they enjoy in their own lives.
- Never hesitate to share your excitement and joy with them, even though they may not overtly show theirs to you.

Managing Drainers
- Establish clear boundaries for the relationship.
- Keep the time you share to a minimum.
- Manage your energy reserves in advance of your time together so as not to be overwhelmed by their negativity.

START TODAY!

1. Clip photos of people and activities that propel you to your best self and toward your dreams. Add these to your *Me File.*
2. Describe how you feel when you are with your Propellers or engaged in "propelling" activities.
3. Just for fun—complete one or a number of personality styles quizzes or questionnaires that are available in the reading resources that follow this Chapter. (When you learn about the many personality styles, you learn more about yourself in the process.)

FOR MORE INSPIRATION, DISCOVERY, AND IDEAS

- Biographies and autobiographies of people you admire or respect
- *Personality Types: Using the Enneagram for Self-Discovery* by Don Richard Riso, Russ Hudson (contributor), Houghton Mifflin Co., 1996
- *Please Understand Me: Character and Temperament Types* by David Kiersey, Marilyn Bates, Prometheus Nemesis Book Co., 1984
- *The Artist's Way: A Spiritual Path to Higher Creativity* by Julia Cameron, JP Tarcher, 1992

- *The Dance of Connections: How to Talk to Someone When You're Mad, Hurt, Scared, Frustrated, Insulted, Betrayed or Desperate* by Harriet Lerner, Ph.D., HarperCollins, 2001
- *The Secret Language of Relationships: Your Complete Personology Guide to Any Relationship with Anyone* by Gary Goldschneider, Joost Elffers, Penguin Studio, 1997

6

Your Social Self

YOUR PUBLIC PERSONA

- "Should I walk over and introduce myself?"
- "Do I kiss, bow, or shake hands?"
- "Which bread plate is mine?"
- "Should I send a thank you note?"
- "Which fork should I use?"
- "Where do I leave my napkin if I get up to use the restroom?"
- "Am I obligated to send a gift?"
- "Must I invite her on-again, off-again beau?"
- "Who should pay the check?"

I am not an Athenian or a Greek, but a citizen of the world.

—*Socrates, Greek philosopher*

The questions go on and on. Some social situations are challenging, while others throw us so far off balance that recovering seems impossible. And etiquette is even more complex in today's global environment. (Some cultures, for instance, have an entire set of appropriate behaviors surrounding the exchange of business cards.)

Then, of course, there are the "gems" that escape our lips when we're not looking…

- "When is the baby due?" *Oh, you're not pregnant. I see.*
- "Did I have this piece of lettuce in my teeth the whole time I was talking with the President of the company?" *Yes you did.*

61

- "Oh, dear, was that your salad I just ate?" *Sorry.*
- "Oh, please, let me help you clean up that glass of red wine I just spilled on your new white carpet." *Oops, I guess I'll never be invited back here.*
- "Cheryl, your grandmother is calling you." *Oh, that's your mother. Yes, I see the resemblance now.*

In the seconds following a gaffe, we desperately try to think of ways to yank the foot out of our mouth or be swallowed by the Earth. Red faced, palms sweating, we back away making apologetic noises and head for the nearest exit.

"It's one thing to design my image, and work on my appearance, my home, and my relationships," one of my students once told me, "but to take my 'self' out in public? That's a little more than I can manage sometimes."

One thing is certain: EVERYONE suffers from some degree of anxiety about social situations, whether it's a business meeting, dinner with a friend we haven't seen in years, or the event that scores highest on the gaffe potential scale: a wedding.

Of course, personal dignity is only one casualty of improper etiquette. Social mistakes have a range of consequences: they may offend people, damage relationships or cost you the job, the raise, the promotion, or the sale.

The worst case scenario is the gaffe you don't even recognize. Remember when your neighbor told you her weight and you responded with, "Really? That's great! You look much heavier!" Or when you were invited to visit your colleague's new home and said, "Your new house is lovely. It's such an improvement over your last place!"

Yet, as fraught and arcane as proper etiquette can be, there is no scientific evidence to prove that anyone has actually died from embarrassment (though there are times when we may wish we could).

Etiquette Matters

For most of us, the word *etiquette* conjures up images of a grandmother sipping tea in white gloves, pinky well-extended. In reality, etiquette today is far more evolved, practical, and all-encompassing than in Granny's day.

Bear in mind that your public persona isn't confined to social or business situations. The minute you behave at all, in any setting, you've displayed your social self, and that's the you others will remember.

Thus, by definition, your public persona is the sum total of the behaviors you exhibit in the company of others. Etiquette, also referred to as manners or, according to entertainment publicist and communicator extraordinaire, Michael Levine, your "Social IQ" is the central element of your public persona. It is simply another way of expressing empathy, awareness, and concern for the comfort of others in your company. As manners expert and etiquette icon Emily Post put it: "Manners are a sensitive awareness of the feelings of others. If you have that awareness, you have good manners, no matter what fork you use."

A comforting thought, but we still want to know what fork we *should* be using. (For a detailed guide on dining etiquette, see: *Emily Post's Etiquette, 75th Anniversary*, HarperCollins, 1997.)

We look with envy upon those who always seem to know what to do or how to smooth over missteps with aplomb. How have they honed these social skills? Most likely through some combination of observation, reading, and yes, experiences…the good, the bad, and the really bad.

A while back, I was preparing to present at a luncheon for an executive group. From the distance of the podium, I noticed that one of the staff had taken his seat and proceeded to eat the bread off the plate of the place to his right, the seat of the Department Head. I quietly signaled to the maitre d' to replace the bread. Thinking all was well, I started my talk, only to see the man do the same thing again!

The next morning, the unwitting bread thief called to say he had received a note that read, *It was lovely to see you at the luncheon yesterday. Please join me for a private dining tutorial at...* "Lauren, you're the business etiquette expert," he said. "What did I do wrong?"

He confided that despite his success (at 28, he was already a Vice President), he was never comfortable in social situations. He was beginning to recognize the very real possibility that this lack of knowledge and skill would hold back his otherwise promising career. With some guidance, he has since become an active ambassador of informed social self-awareness.

Learning the Ropes Proper etiquette starts with a willingness to learn the rules and an appreciation of the cost if we ignore them. (Refer to the end of this chapter for additional resources for this information.)

Next is experience. Don't avoid social situations simply because you think you'll be uncomfortable. Trust yourself and take a leap of faith. With some of the basics under your belt, chances are you'll surpass your own expectations and feel better about the next time.

When accidents happen, a sincere apology, an effort to help or make amends, or a genuine smile can quickly diffuse tension and immediately make someone feel more comfortable. A sense of humor is invaluable...the ability to laugh at your own mistake may be the perfect antidote for discomfort or embarrassment.

Each of these tools will move you closer to the ultimate goal of presenting to the world your best self in all aspects of your life.

START TODAY!

Take out your *Me File*.
1. List five social situations in which you most frequently find yourself, such as restaurants, black tie events, cocktail receptions, entertaining business clients, colleagues or friends.
2. Describe a social situation (or many situations) that left you asking, "What should I have done?"
3. Describe how you actually handled each of the above situations.
4. Are you satisfied with your response or would you have done something different based on the information you have today?

FOR MORE INSPIRATION, DISCOVERY, AND IDEAS

Contact The Association of Image Consultants International at www.aici.org or call toll-free (877) 247-3319.

- *Raise Your Social IQ* by Michael Levine, Carol Publishing Group, 1998
- *The Idiot's Guide to Etiquette* by Mary Mitchell with John Corr, Alpha Books, 1996
- *Managing Your Mouth* by Robert L. Genua, AMACOM, 1992
- *Kiss, Bow or Shake Hands* (International Etiquette) by Terri Morrison, Wayne Conaway and George A. Borden, Ph.D., Bob Adams, Inc., 1994
- *Multicultural Manners—New Rules of Etiquette for a Changing Society* (International Etiquette) by John Mole, John Wiley & Sons, Inc., 1996
- *Everyday Etiquette (Emily Post's Essentials)* by Peggy Post, Harper Mass Market Paperbacks, 1999

Your Work

Dream the Impossible Dream

What if you allowed yourself to dream the impossible? Bernadette Grey, former Editor-in-Chief of *Working Woman* magazine, asks colleagues and friends to consider two questions:

1. "What did you want to be when you grew up?" and
2. "Are you making your living doing what you love to do?"

Such questions! Surely it's impossible to become what you always dreamed or earn a living doing what you love to do. It would be beyond anyone's wildest dreams to expect such things.

Or would it?

Results of a pre-college vocational exam decreed that based on my natural talents, skills, likes, and dislikes, I was suited to be a social worker, an attorney, or a florist. Since I'd always dreamed of being an attorney, that was no surprise. But I had never considered social work, despite my joy and sense of fulfillment from working with children and the elderly. And a florist? Flowers have always been gifts for the people I love and colorful home decorations that create beauty and joy, not a profession.

"Advance confidently in the direction of your own dreams and endeavor to live the life that you have imagined."

— Henry David Thoreau, author, philosopher, naturalist

Needless to say, I paid no attention to the results of this exam.

67

I went to work, lived abroad, and let life happen without any particular outline or plan. Apparently, I had to do some living before my real direction would become clear.

In my early 30s, I decided to pursue a graduate degree in business. There, my heart and mind were forever changed by a marketing class assignment to create the business of my dreams.

I built a business around my favorite sports: taking friends shopping, showing them how to select and apply make-up, and helping them style their hair. To complete the assignment, I developed a financial plan that detailed how my hypothetical business could turn a profit providing these services.

From that moment on, it was full steam ahead. That little business plan actually contained the seeds of my image consulting and writing practice, as well as the fulfillment of the prophecy of that vocational exam so many years before.

Today, I encourage my clients and students to build their images and enhance their lives (social worker); I influence through language and logical process (attorney); and I work with things of beauty that inspire happiness and make people-smile (florist). My days have been made richer, joy-filled, in fact, through the marriage of my passions and my skills. Such a relationship provides a unique connection to one's work.

My work is truly a part of who I am…and vice versa. This can be true for you as well.

YOUR PASSION

Whether you're a teacher, homemaker, consultant, artist, or corporate executive, when you bring your passion and your talent to your work, you experience a new level of enjoyment and *you make a contribution by simply being who you are.* Every day, you bring your ideas, insights and solutions into being. You autograph your work with your originality, flair, humor, and sense of style. You come to understand the difference between "work" and "a labor of love."

Where do your passions and talents intersect? This often takes some soul-searching and deep thought...

- Be patient and be open. Like any important life-changing discovery, you may need to look beyond the obvious to see clearly.

- Don't look back. History does not predict your future. Look out to the horizon, and remember, the journey is yours to design.

- Ask trusted friends, family, and colleagues to share what they believe your natural talents to be. You will surely find many unexpected pleasant surprises and ideas.

- Think outside the box. Don't design yourself into another corporate job just because you've always had one. Don't continue starving to make it as an artist if there are other paths that move you to joy. Conventional wisdom says we must find the one form of work that will sustain us, our energy, and our interests forever. But who says you can't rewrite the wisdom of our age?

Today, it's highly unusual to hear about someone celebrating 25, 30, or 40 years with one company. Mostly you hear, "He's owns a gallery now. Before that he was a teacher. He once sold insurance. He's also an ordained minister, and he's written a few travel books!" People are doing so much more today than in the past by simply connecting their minds and their hearts to their work. Break out! Be one of them.

Richard

Richard was one of the sweetest, kindest souls I had ever met. His goodness and his gentle nature almost entered a room before him. This coupled with his many academic degrees should have guaranteed Richard a power position in his field. Nevertheless, after years of disappointment at the hands of unskilled managers, Richard knew it was time to look for a new position outside his company. He had been recommended to me by the university and had no idea what to expect.

At our first meeting, Richard was very reserved and proper. His *Me File* showed a person quite different from the one I met. The inner Richard, I discovered, was artistic, creative, and colorful. However, to accommodate his professional self, Richard had put his true self away. He hid behind pale gray suits and shirts and oversized eyeglasses. It wasn't until weeks into our work that Richard admitted that he had always longed to be an artist; that as a child, he was at his happiest in the basement sculpting or painting.

Richard's parents feared that he would struggle as they had to earn a living and insisted that he give up his passion and accept the "real world," which when translated meant: to pursue a "real" profession. As a result, Richard's artistic passions and talents were put aside while he earned two degrees in science, a law degree and an MBA. Richard also earned the right to be officially miserable. His whole world was in conflict. Richard could not see a way to live his passion and earn a living to support his family. He had created a false professional persona that conflicted with the things he loved the most.

Slowly we worked together to integrate some color and style into Richard's very gray wardrobe. We found stylish accessories that had an artistic quality that he genuinely appreciated. We assessed Richard's verbal communications and started to rehearse conversations that talked about things outside his professional and industry topics. We enrolled Richard in a yoga class to start reconnecting his mind, his body, and his spirit.

He began to investigate organizations and activities that moved him and fed his spirit. He described his passions and interests to everyone he met and volunteered his services where he would feel that he added value. One day, he received a call inviting him to become the executive director of one of those organizations. He accepted.

Richard's wife now comes home to a man who sings to himself and smiles. They laugh more and worry less. His children see a man who was willing to look into himself and understand that unless he changed, nothing in his life would change.

"MY WORK/MY SELF"

Take out your *Me File* and get ready to work. This activity is called *My Work/My Self.*

Begin by writing your answers to these questions—
1. "What did you want to be when you grew up?"
2. "What activities—paid or unpaid—do you love and enjoy most?"

Next, list—
- the five things you value most in life
- the five things you value most in work
- three activities that make you feel most creative, challenged, and productive
- two to three passions or hobbies
- three people who share your interests
- three people you've helped over the years
- three topics you know a lot about. For each, list—
  - three audiences that might be interested in paying for this information
  - three businesses that hire and pay specialists to provide this information

Finally, rate the following from least to most important to you in a work situation (1=Most Important; 8=Least Important)—

- Money
- Structured work day
- Professional environment
- Excitement
- Casual dress
- Team participation
- Flexible time
- Independence

Look at the top four items on your list. Does your current work offer all, some, or none of them?

Next Steps Complete all the exercises. Then take a break. Let the dust settle a bit. Get a cup of coffee or go for a walk.

Return and review your answers. Is there a picture developing in your mind?

Can you envision work that blends your natural talents, interests, and passions?

For instance, if you love gardening and you are a talented writer, can you start a gardening newsletter in your community? Submit articles to *House and Garden* magazine? Create a website of creative gardening tips for avid gardeners, offering valuable "How-To" guides for beginners?

If you enjoy cooking and you love to teach, would you consider creating cooking seminars in a local bookstore or at the library? Could you co-sponsor these seminars with the cable food channel or a local restaurant? How about selling a deck of your favorite recipe cards to people who attend?

Perhaps you're like Stephanie, whose *My Work/My Self* activity revealed her love for public relations and sports. She knew the names, statistics and histories of every player in the NFL. Through *My Work/My Self*, she identified television and the Internet as businesses that hire specialists in this area. She also realized how much she craved the professional companionship and energy of a young, exciting team.

After completing the exercise, it took just three phone calls for Stephanie to land her dream job: in public relations for NFL.com. She was, and continues to be, ecstatic.

THE BRAND CALLED YOU

Say CAR. Note what comes to mind.

Now say MERCEDES. What comes to mind? Something a bit different.

Say HAMBURGER.

Now say MCDONALD'S. Big difference, right?

The difference is branding and image.

As it is with objects and food, so it is with people. In short, your image matters. From Tony Bennett to Apple Computer, billions of dollars are spent each year to build images through brand messages.

How about you? Your brand message is built on what I call the three V's:

YOUR VISUAL APPEARANCE, YOUR VISUAL AIDS, AND YOUR VERBAL SKILLS

Your Visual Appearance Does your look say you are the very best at what you do? If you're in business, are you polished and sharp (a crisp suit, perhaps a tie, freshly polished, well-groomed shoes, flattering hair and make-up, sharp accessories to complete your look)? If you're a homemaker, do you pull yourself together every day, style your hair, apply even minimal make-up, and wear something other than sweats? If you're self-employed, does your look introduce your message? Does it reflect your clients and prospects? Are you neither under- nor over-done?

Your Visual Aids These include your—
- business cards
- personal note cards
- promotional materials
- resume
- portfolio

Are they simple, sharp, and appropriate? Do they present the image you want to portray to your clients, colleagues, and your self?

73

Your Verbal Skills
These include your—
- tone of voice
- choice of words
- enunciation
- powers of description
- listening skills
- facial animation
- appropriate use of language to persuade, motivate, explain, or entertain

Do you have a powerful command of language? Have you developed your listening skills, your ability to read your audience and anticipate their information needs? Can you describe a scene so clearly that your listener believes he was there with you? Do you use your facial expression and the pace and tone of your speech to keep listeners engaged?

To harness the power of the brand called you, each tool must function as a building block, supporting the foundation necessary for your unique brand and your successful image.

START TODAY!

1. Talk to five people you know who appear to love their work. Ask them:
   - How they initially discovered this work
   - What they did to get to where they are today
   - What they believe to be your greatest strengths and talents
   - What profession or line of work they see you best suited for
2. Compare their answers with your thoughts about yourself and your responses to the *My Work/My Self* activity.
3. Add their responses and insights to the *My Work/My Self* activity in your *Me File.*

FOR MORE INSPIRATION, DISCOVERY, AND IDEAS

- *Do What You Are: Discover the Perfect Career for You Through the Secrets of Personality Type* by Paul D. Tieger, Barbara Barron-Tieger, Little Brown and Company, 2001
- *Maximum Achievement* by Brian Tracy, Fireside, 1995
- *The Brand You 50 Or Fifty Ways to Transform Yourself from an "Employee" into a Brand That Shouts Distinction, Commitment, and Passion!* by Tom Peters, Knopf, 1999
- *Now, Discover Your True Strengths* by Marcus Buckingham, Donald O. Clifton, Ph.D., Free Press, 2001

Your Image, Your Life

"You are the CEO of your life," the ad for Discover Brokerage proclaims. Unlike the jobs you've had, this one is different. This time IT'S YOUR NAME ON THE DOOR. And this isn't a dress rehearsal...every night is opening night.

Image determines how you see yourself, and ultimately, how the world sees you. This means that your entire life depends on the clarity, consistency, and quality of your image. When you cultivate this image deliberately and strategically, all doors will open before you. The key words are "deliberately and strategically." In other words, take your time.

You may have heard the saying, "A journey of 1,000 miles begins with a single step." What they don't tell you is how tough that first step is...how hard it is to break old patterns and habits as you begin to create and recreate your authentic self, your personal best.

Here's the good news: you've already taken that first step. In the simple act of opening this book, even if all you've done is flip through the pages and read a paragraph or two, you're on your way.

Congratulations and bon voyage in creating your authentic, unique, and very personal best.

Instant Image Matters!

Even if you take just a few moments to consider these questions and the activities, you will have taken the first step on your journey to your personal best…because it truly only takes an instant for your image to matter.

1: Your Self

- Do you live your life on purpose and with a purpose?
- Is your attitude an asset or a liability?

List five ways your attitude impacts how you feel at the end of the day.

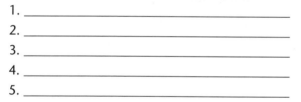

1. _____
2. _____
3. _____
4. _____
5. _____

2: Your Appearance

- Do you look and feel great every time you walk out your door?
- Can you easily see all the clothes in your closet and put together a "magic outfit" everyday?

List five ways your appearance impacts your day.

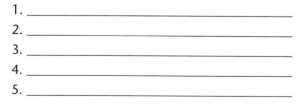

1. _____
2. _____
3. _____
4. _____
5. _____

3: Your Physical Health

- Have you had a complete physical evaluation in the last year?

- Could you eat a more healthful diet and add 10 minutes of exercise to each day?

List five ways you could improve your physical condition and thereby improve your life.

1. _____
2. _____
3. _____
4. _____
5. _____

4: Your Home

- Take a walk through your home. In which room do you feel best?
- What is it about that room that is different from the rest? Is it the colors? The furnishings? The accessories?

List five things you can do in your home to make every room warm, welcoming, and comfortable to you.

1. _____
2. _____
3. _____
4. _____
5. _____

5: Your Relationships

- Who are/were the people who helped you get to where you are today? Who were the positive, formative influences in your life? I call these your Propellers.
- Who are the people who drain your energy, who keep you off balance and unsure of yourself? I call these your Drainers.

List five ways your Propeller relationships have served you or cost you.

1. _____
2. _____
3. _____
4. _____
5. _____

Instant Image Matters!

List five ways your Drainer relationships have served you or cost you.

1. _____
2. _____
3. _____
4. _____
5. _____

6: Your Social Self

- Have you ever avoided a social situation because you felt uncomfortable or awkward?
- Have you ever been in a situation that left you asking "What should I have done?"

List five social gaffes you've committed and how you would handle them differently today, given the information you now have. Hindsight is after all 20/20.

1. _____
2. _____
3. _____
4. _____
5. _____

7: Your Work

- Does your current work situation maximize a blend of your natural talents, interests, and passions?
- When people think of you, does your personal brand immediately support your desired message?

List five words you would like people to use when describing you.

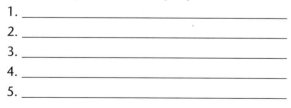

1. _____
2. _____
3. _____
4. _____
5. _____

On Your Own, But Not Alone

If you've started along your way but stalled in the middle or if you're enjoying the journey and would like a partner to travel with you, contact the Association of Image Consultants International. Many hundreds of image professionals from around the world would be happy to work with you at all points on the journey to your best self.

The Association of Image Consultants International
2695 Villa Creek Drive, Suite 260
Dallas, TX 75234
Call toll free: 877.247.3319
Email: info@aici.org
Visit the web site at: www.aici.org